S0-FLO-420

"Do not blame Caesar, blame the people of Rome who have so enthusiastically acclaimed and adored him and rejoiced in their loss of freedom and danced in his path and gave him triumphal processions and laughed delightedly at his licentiousness and thought it very superior of him to acquire vast amounts of gold illicitly. Blame the people who hail him when he speaks in the Forum of the 'new, wonderful good society' which shall now be Rome's, interpreted to mean 'more money, more ease, more security, more living fatly at the expense of the industrious.' Julius was always an ambitious villain, but he is only one man."

Marcus Tullius Cicero

Red State Coalition
(Vermont Not to be Excluded)

Written by Americans

copyright 2010 by

Americans of the Red State Coalition and FMK Firearms

www.fmkfirearms.com

www.formykountry.com

www.redstatecoalition.com

ISBN 978-1-61658-913-4

Published by Jim

Edited by Adrienne and Laurel (just in case there are typos or bad grammar, blame them.)

Printed in the United States of America—Proudly

First Edition

Contents

Introduction		1
Red and Blue	by RSP	5
Different but United	by SMC	15
Federalism—RIP	by RWR	23
Wealth	by RHL	29
Property	by JKP	34
Life	by KMP	37
God	by LEW	39
Amendment Number Two	by DRW	42
Accomplishment, Honor and Virtue	by GLB	47
Constitutional Contortionists	by RHL	50
Palin-ology	by SMC	54
The General United Electric States of America	by GLB	57
I...American	by PVJ	60
RSC Flag	by Paige	64
The Government We Deserve	by AHC	65
Liberty or Tyranny	by KMP	68
A New Declaration		70
Declaration of Independence		73
Constitution of the United States		80
Notes		108
About the Authors (on back cover)		

This book is dedicated to all the Americans bent out of shape and fit to be tied to a Federal Government that has no interest in the best well being of its citizens.

Introduction

The United States of America is at a crossroads. Our current president and legislature, continuing on an ideological arc set by many presidents and many legislatures is taking our nation, this freest nation, this most benevolent nation, and this most productive nation, down a path where the individual liberty and unmatched prosperity, unique to our country, shall cease to exist.

This transformation is not occurring without division. While many citizens have become complacent, willing to except despotic rule by corporate and political oligarchy, and have succumbed to utopian promises of "universal health care", "clean energy", and the abstract concept of a "compassionate and fair" America, those blessed with analytical thinking skills know intuitively, and from history, that all promises of utopia end in dictatorship.

The American spirit is resistant, and will not tolerate this destructive march toward collective governance.

American apprehension toward this movement transcends political party and ideology.

The political class has joined forces with the most powerful corporations in the nation to maintain a status quo where those who prosper will not do so by satisfying market (and therefore individual) demands, but by paying tribute and loyalty to the political powers that be.

The recent Congressional spectacles that rush not billions, but *trillions* of taxpayer dollars into even more clandestine control alarm many; yet not enough of our American citizens.

This divide cannot be reconciled by political remedy. Given that our politicians have adeptly pitted classes, races, and regions, against each other for personal gain; many of us no longer view ourselves as simply "American," but of some sort of American:

African-American, Asian-American, Hispanic-American, sometimes just—Hard-Working American.

What's worse, the parasitic political class has convinced those of one group that those of another group are responsible for their misfortune.

In recent public statements, Texas Governor Rick Perry, suggested, in a round-about way, that secession could be a just action and remedy to combat an overbearing Federal Government. Geraldo Rivera, the Fox News contributor, nearly had an apoplectic meltdown at the thought that someone as lofty as State Governor might make such an implication, suggesting the Governor was wandering into kooky "fringe" land.

It was quite a display and the level of intensity and disapproval in Geraldo's disdain was unsettling for those who agreed with the Governor's sentiments. Especially, considering the Governor only insinuated that secession "might" be a possible remedy for an over-bearing Federal Government bent on impinging State sovereignty.

Meanwhile, many of us uncultured pedestrian people were screaming, "Secede, Secede, Secede!"

If Geraldo thought Governor Perry was a "fringe" lunatic for suggesting secession as a "possible" reasonable course to combat unreasonable government, then what would he consider us TV watching, "Secede, Secede, Secede", screaming American citizens?

Complete whack jobs one would suppose.

We really couldn't tune in to Geraldo's disdain. Why would loyal Americans not wish to secede from a nation that has already seceded from the principles of freedom and liberty that our nation's Founders so diligently fought for?

If the United States Government chooses not to honor those concepts enshrined within our Constitution then why would we Americans fight to keep this union together?

We have written this little booklet not to encourage the destruction of the United States, but to ask fellow Americans to consider how maintaining the political structure of all our undivided states today threatens America. We propose not to disassemble America, but to bring together a coalition of States that wish to protect the liberties and freedoms of "the People" as envisioned by our Founders. We propose that our Federal Government's only charter be to protect and guarantee those liberties and freedoms under the Constitution of the United States, as originally was its responsibility.

If some citizens believe the federal power should have no limits, and that government ought to necessarily reinterpret law and limit freedom, to achieve ends irreconcilable with a textual understanding of our law, then we propose those citizens assemble the States happy under our current federal power and continue the status quo. Conversely, our new nation, a Red State Coalition, shall construct a new Federal Government dedicated to our law as it is written. We will happily reside side by side as two nations.

We are all citizens of the United States and yet many do not want to maintain or protect American values and principles, as intended by our Founding Fathers, and wish to promote a new order. Our country cannot survive such drastic and severe philosophical differences as one entity.

A two-state solution is not suggested to promote conflict. It is envisioned to allow those who embrace philosophies not of our Founder's intent, to flourish or fail under our current union, and allow those wishing to restore American principles to exist under a new one.

What follows is an examination of founding principles, with contemporary illustration, that shows how our political elite have forsaken successful ideologies for utopian ones; which history reminds us have never succeeded.

Recognizing the cultural divide integrated into our nation by ignoble politicians and malevolent clandestine organizations, we believe a two-state solution for America is the only one that will allow a peaceful transition for our country. Not making this transition is certain to drive us down a path where increased conflict and disharmony will assure our mutual destruction.

Written by Americans
July 4, 2009

Red and Blue   by RSP

The whole point of democracy is to allow the People to have a voice in determining their own futures. The point of Republican government is to insure that voice does not become so loud as to trample the rights and Natural Laws intuitive to mankind.

In searching for a motto to distinguish our nation, the Founders selected "E Pluribus Unum"—from many one.

We are one nation from many nationalities, backgrounds and experiences, yet we share a "oneness" that binds us into a singular culture with straight forward and simple aim—Life and Liberty shall not be subjugated to the whim of government.

In a fledgling nation populated by sturdy individuals fleeing Europe, our early settlers, though varying in background, were bound up by the similar experience of religious persecution. They appreciated passionately the luxury of liberty. This shared passion more than made up for the strife that might have occurred from religious differences.

Brutally contentious, vulgar, and aggressive, America's early elections were every bit as dirty as we see today; this contention, however, focused on how to best secure Liberty and not on how to best thwart it.

The whole concept of liberty has evolved and become distorted to mean something completely different than its dictionary definition, which simply is—freedom for individuals to pursue their own will unmolested by government.

Adept politicians, with poetic and charismatic oratory, have used the concept of "liberty" to seize for themselves more dictatorial control over citizens, and have done so by claiming these new powers on behalf of the American people.

In perhaps one of the best examples of American demagoguery, our 32nd President, Franklin Delano Roosevelt, addressed Congress on January 6, 1941 with a famous oration that became known as the "Four Freedoms" speech. Near the end of his speech he summarized with this:

"In the future days, which we seek to make secure, we look forward to a world founded upon four essential human freedoms.

The first is freedom of speech and expression—everywhere in the world.

The second is freedom of every person to worship God in his own way—everywhere in the world.

The third is freedom from want—which, translated into world terms, means economic understandings which will secure to every nation a healthy peacetime life for its inhabitants—everywhere in the world.

The fourth is freedom from fear—which, translated into world terms, means a world-wide reduction of armaments to such a point and in such a thorough fashion that no nation will be in a position to commit an act of physical aggression against any neighbor—anywhere in the world.

That is no vision of a distant millennium. It is a definite basis for a kind of world attainable in our own time and generation."

By combining freedom from fear and freedom from want with the admired and treasured rights of speech and religion, Roosevelt shrewdly invites Americans into a new kind of thinking. If protecting the American citizen from want and fear become within the purview of our Federal Government, then what powers will be allotted to government to carry out this charter?

Clearly Americans were not alleviated from "fear" in the spirit that Roosevelt spoke of in his generation, the next generation, or even the next. To suggest that he even believed such worldwide control was possible illustrates extreme naiveté or astute knowledge that the "fear of fear" would give him the public support he needed to proceed with his agenda.

The freedom from "want" is an even more esoteric concept. How do we possibly characterize it? If I "want" a Lamborghini, does that mean government should provide it for me?

Of course "want", as defined in the bureaucratic mind, would be credited by government edict. Roosevelt's whole intent in articulating the philosophy was not to eliminate want; it was to empower government and to forever distort the meaning of Liberty.

Following up on his New Deal, many policies of which were overturned by the Supreme Court, Roosevelt's strategy was to take his case directly to the people, promising that government should answer individual desires.

The "Four Freedoms" speech could very well demarcate the point in American history where the rugged individualism that defined Americans would forever acquiesce to a more helpless and needy citizenry, and so much the better for the progressive movement's intent to shift power from individual citizens to government.

Today the media presents this demarcation each election by painting some States Red and some Blue. These electoral maps consistently show a predictable divide between the coasts and Middle America but they do not adequately reveal who *is* Blue and who *is* Red.

Without too much analysis it is pretty easy to figure out who is who.

Members of the Blue camp overwhelmingly benefit when government regulation and policy skew the playing field so that excellence is *not* used as supreme arbiter of reward. Lawyers, Union Workers, Government Workers, Wage Earners below the 50% mark who pay no income taxes, Big Business, Celebrities, and Wall Street all find their loyalties reside with Democrats and those wishing for more government power and control.

Red camp members overwhelmingly are small business owners, entrepreneurs, independent doctors, key employees, managers (in the higher income brackets who actually pay taxes), and those young driven Americans who believe that *their* futures and *their* good fortunes reside within *their* ability to compete in a free market and succeed by achieving excellence in *their* endeavors.

Red Camp members like head to head competition on a level playing field, Blue Camp members don't.

Lawyers: Just about every American business activity is more expensive because of lawyers and that means costs to consumers are greater. When Barack Obama spoke in front of the American Medical Association (not exactly a conservative group) and declared he would not support any cap on jury awards which are responsible for many out of control costs in health care, the audience moaned a collective sigh of disgust. Malpractice insurance is one of the healthcare industry's most draconian costs, and while the President complains about the cost of healthcare, he avoids the simplest and most effective method to help control it—tort reform.

A lawyer can sue anyone at anytime for any reason with very little fear of consequence. Sensible countries have instituted "loser-pays" where plaintiffs can be liable for all legal costs including those incurred by a defendant. These policies severely restrict litigation by unsavory lawyers who have learned to work the system. When lawyers are afraid they might lose that roll of the dice in front of a judge there is a lot more incentive to avoid the frivolous lawsuit.

Lawyers are necessary, but the United States has way too many and their activities add nothing to the productivity of our nation. Their value as "gate keepers" guaranteeing a level playing field has long gone. They are blood-suckers who rob our nation of energy and opportunity. They overwhelmingly support the Blue Camp insuring (given quid pro quo legislation preventing tort reform) that their activities will not be curtailed.

In the Red State Coalition, litigation will be moderated by loser pays!

Union Workers: If union workers believed they could get ahead and prosper through their own diligence and excellence, they wouldn't be in a union. Here is a group who has voluntarily given up individual bargaining rights to some faction because they think they'll do better under some other entity's care than they could do on their own. Having citizens give up personal independence and self-reliance is what the Blue Camp continually endeavors to accomplish.

These guys enthusiastically sacrifice their own God given freedoms because they have convinced themselves some other entity might look out for their best interests better than they would themselves.

How pitiful does one have to become to believe that!

Government Workers: The average government worker makes $65,000; the average worker in private industry makes $48,000. How on earth did that get turned upside down?

When there are 14 million workers in the civil service and you're one of them, who do you vote for, the guy who complains that government is too big or the guy who says he's going to vote for your pay raise?

Government employees are five times more likely to be members of unions than those in the private sector. Weren't unions devised to level the playing field and protect workers from the "evil" robber barons? Isn't it government's job to insure the playing field is level?

Why on earth do individuals working for the organization that is chartered with making sure the playing field is level need to be represented by a union whose job it is to make sure the playing field is level?

It boggles the mind.

Wage Earners below the 50% mark: So you're working twenty-eight hours per week at McDonald's, you've been there for four years and when Barack Obama makes a campaign stop in your town you travel there to ask him what he's going to do to make McDonald's increase your pay.

You've been at McDonald's for four years; WHY IN THE HECK HAVEN'T YOU LEARNED TO RUN THE PLACE ALREADY!

You don't pay any taxes, and, as a matter of fact, many of you actually get back more money than was withheld from your paychecks.

This is corrupt government policy at its best. When you think about it, each election the Blue Camp starts out with half of all votes already in their pocket by promising low wage earners free money. It is amazing that even one Red Camp Member holds public office.

This sort of corrupt buying of votes will be illegal in a Red State Coalition. If you're a member, you must pay something in taxes in proportion to your income, period!

Big Business and Wall Street: With all this talk about Red Campers looking out for big business and always screwing the little guy, why did GE, Warren Buffet, Bill Gates, Google, MGM Grand, Fannie Mae, and Freddie Mac all openly support Obama for president?

And why did Citigroup, JP Morgan Chase, Goldman Sachs, and Morgan Stanley all give two to four times more money to Obama than McCain?

Oh yeah, and why was Hilary Clinton on Wal-Mart's Board of Directors?

Obama and company have taken over Chrysler and General Motors and given a disproportional share of ownership to the Union's (payback for their support), never mind the law, and never mind the little guys with their investments in mutual funds, pension funds, and hedge funds that got Chrysler out of trouble just a year ago.

While not much in this President's administration is transparent, this corrupt patronage is crystal clear. He will use all the government's power to pay those favorable to him, and if "little guys" get smashed in the meantime, so be it.

Red Campers better learn to love Fords now because if GM and Chrysler succeed, it will only encourage more of this kind of corrupt government action in the future.

When government makes rules to regulate business, who do you think is better equipped to deal with that regulation, the big national corporation, or the small businessman with limited resources?

Government regulations effectively close opportunity and make it easier for big business to compete in the marketplace by locking out young entrepreneurs and small businesses with innovative ideas. Imposing severe regulations makes it impossible or too difficult for any "little guy" to comply.

As for billionaires like Warren Buffet and Bill Gates; these guys have extensive control over their incomes and how they obtain them. While they call for higher taxes to suppress the workingman or small business owner (who only makes a moderate salary) by pushing their taxable income rates past the thirty-five percent point, they conveniently rake in their income through capital gains that is taxed at a much lower rate.

On some $50 million in income, poor Warren Buffet paid about 17 percent in income taxes; and this is a guy with a net worth north of $50 billion. This is the definition of "fair" when you're rich and in close proximity to the politicians who make tax policy.

In the Red State Coalition, our public will not be harmed by draconian regulation which kills innovation and creative solutions undermined by government fiat, and we won't tilt the playing field to allow billionaires to screw the rest of us by paying off politicians for preferable tax legislation.

Celebrities: When you make $22 million at 22-years-old because you just happen to secure the lead role in the next fad superhero movie, there is a pretty good chance your thinking is going to get a little off kilter, it doesn't take a genius to recognize that doesn't add up.

"Some people don't make a million dollars their whole working life and that's just not fair!"

"We need to help these poor people and I don't mind paying fifty percent of my 22 million to help, and you're a selfish bastard if you don't give them 50% of your $100,000.00!"

Funny thing about that progressive tax system—it's not really progressive, if it were blockbuster boy would get taxed 50 percent on the first $100,000.00 of that $22 million, 75 percent on the $100,000.00 to one million, 90 percent on the one million to five million, and 99 percent on the five million to 22 million.

Let's try that on for size before we call hard-working guy with the 70-hour workweek a "selfish bastard" because he wants to keep most of his $100,000.00.

The Red Camp: When a progressively smaller and smaller portion of hard working American people find themselves squeezed between titans of business having lunch with politicians, and the "poor" (which has become half the nation) being leveraged by politicians for their own ends, there is no representation to be amassed that can protect their interests.

When Constitutional protections are ignored by interpreting them to be "obsolete" for our modern world, the only recourse this group has is to leave.

Unlike those in the preceding enumeration, we Red Campers are motivated to obtain prosperity through our own hard work and want nothing that we didn't earn. We have no desire to subjugate or to suppress opponents through government intervention. We know prosperity is greatest when all members of society succeed or fail by providing goods and services other members of society desire without the tumultuous, arbitrary, and artificial demands set forth by corrupt government.

We wish well the lawyers, union workers, government workers, low-wage earners, big businesses, celebrities and Wall Street members who have found such comfortable opportunity in the United States where politicians have designed their advantage, but we do not wish to support them through authoritarian rule that allows them to unfairly benefit from our works.

We want to leave because we value American individualism and culture.

We will not be adverse to *free* trade and we will happily keep our borders open to Blue Camp groups wishing to trade with our small business owners, entrepreneurs, and doctors.

Our only stipulation will be that you all go home when you're done because we don't want you destroying the opportunities we provide our young driven Americans who believe that their futures and their fortunes reside within their ability to achieve excellence, and not within their ability to pay obsequious homage to Monarchial politicians.

Different but United   by SMC

Those of us in the kooky "fringe" who have considered secession as a viable and reasonable tack to take have not come to this conclusion because we wish to destroy America, but rather, we have come to it because we want America back. We believe the Federal Government has subverted the People's will and has not endeavored to protect the People's rights. Furthermore, we believe the Federal Government has designed and promoted a bureaucracy unelected and unaccountable that persists with no consideration for the People's freedoms. We believe an orderly and united secession movement is the only way to affect a transfer of power from the despotic rulers within our Federal Government, its bureaucracies, and its agencies, to the People and States; the only just repository for that power.

Group vs. Individual State Secession: Pound for pound the hyena has the most powerful jaws of any mammal. It is quite a formidable and capable hunter all on its own, and yet, the hyena hunts in a pack. Hyenas have been known to take down and consume seemingly invincible large lions and tigers. We Americans might learn something in studying the hyena.

Many States are beginning to develop vigorous and robust secession movements and any one State could possibly succeed in such a quest, however, secession is not the real goal for these movements. The real goal is simply to restore freedom.

What politicians have been very adept at doing has been to highlight differences among us to get *"We the People"* to fight amongst ourselves, so we unwittingly sacrifice our freedoms and our liberties to government authority. Recognition of this and recognition that together, though different, we are invincible, the federal authority will have to bow to our will.

What we need to succeed in taking our power back is a national secession movement amongst our likeminded states that can emphasize our desire for individual liberty and deemphasize the differences that cause us to be divided and, in turn, vulnerable to federal rule.

Because we believe our current Federal Government will never relinquish its power over us and will only become more tyrannical in its evolution, the first order of business for a Red State Coalition would be to organize the several states most dedicated to freedom and liberty as outlined in our Founding documents and combine their political power to tell Washington DC, "No More!"!

No more tax revenue will be relinquished to the Federal Government, no more participation in the bankrupt programs that must steal from our younger generations to finance the older ones and no more tolerance for tyrannical rule clearly in violation of our supreme law.

Conceiving "no more to the Federal Government" is a much simpler concept to *say* than to *do*. Given the unavoidable complications that will arise forsaking the federal revenue and structure that supports citizens throughout the nation with Social Security, Medicare, and other federal programs there is cause for concern, but we must recognize, these systems *are* going to fail anyway. The federal remedy for this failure is surely to be even more onerous and burdensome than what is tolerated today.

The important concept to gain is; the better we organize now for the impending separation, the better we will be prepared to operate a successful new entity that is not fearful of the federal power or the complications inherent to the separation.

The key is our likeminded states must join forces to forge a stronger union than might be achieved by remaining separate entities. At one time, the United States did benefit from a synergetic bond that occurred due to cooperation of the several States, but today, the benefits of our amalgamation seem trite and departed.

In the tradition of our Founding, we must emphasize that which is most important—the preservation of our inalienable rights and freedoms, and deemphasize those passionate issues that politicians have used to divide us.

Following are a few examples that illustrate how seemingly contradictory entities may have more in common than not, and how combining efforts for a similar goal will bring more success than might be achieved by driving toward the same goal separately.

Vermont and Texas: In order to successfully promote a two state solution, it is important that the individual states understand who their allies are and who they are not. The answer is not found in left/right politics, it is found in free/not free politics, or it is found in less government instead of more government politics.

At first glance it may appear that the political positions associated with southern conservative states like Texas are totally incompatible with some of the political positions associated with northern liberal states like Vermont. On closer examination, it becomes evident that these states share much more ideological common ground than the media might lead you to believe.

Regarding the 2nd Amendment for example:

In Texas is there a waiting period on gun sales? No
In Texas are handgun buyers required to complete safety training? No
In Texas is it required that you register all of your guns with law enforcement? No
In Texas are background checks required at gun shows? No
In Texas do state police and federal NICS perform a background check? No
In Texas is it mandatory that locking devices be sold with guns? No
In Texas is a license or permit required to buy handguns? No
In Texas are background checks required on "private" gun sales? No
In Texas are there any restrictions regarding minors possessing guns? Yes
In Texas may the police limit carrying concealed handguns? No

In Vermont is there a waiting period on gun sales? No
In Vermont are handgun buyers required to complete safety training? No
In Vermont is it required that you register all of your guns with law enforcement? No
In Vermont are background checks required at gun shows? No
In Vermont do state police and federal NICS perform a background check? Yes
In Vermont is it mandatory that locking devices be sold with guns? No
In Vermont is a license or permit required to buy handguns? No
In Vermont are background checks required on "private" gun sales? No
In Vermont are there any restrictions regarding minors possessing guns? Yes
In Vermont may the police limit carrying concealed handguns? No

Try this survey in Illinois or New York and see how many yes's you get!

When we investigate which states have an active and robust secession movement we find Vermont and Texas lead the pack. Despite the fact that one is described as far *left* and one is described as far *right*, the two states are much more similar than they are different. What they really desire is freedom and they both abhor the despotic power of the Federal Government.

In fact, when analyzing policy at the state level and when questioning citizens "on the ground," there are only a few states that portend they would prefer more government control and service at the sacrifice of freedom (despite what General Colin Powell says). When citizens are queried directly, even in the largest and poorest metropolitan areas where voters are notoriously known to lean left, they too opt for "conservative" positions when pressed on issues where personal freedoms are concerned.

Actually, to maintain our united front and promote our agenda, "conservative" should not be used in such political discourse. Because right and left have been delineated by politicians to strategically distract us from *their* goals—to bolster *their* power and *their* control over us—we should learn to think and speak in terms of free and not free. Each time politicians get more power, more ability to legislate, and more of our money, we become less free.

Whether or not Texas is conservative, or Vermont is liberal, they both have something much bigger and much more important in common, they want local control over their destiny and they don't want the Federal Government telling them what to do.

Slavery, 1776: Each generation has had to contend with the practical realities which plague political negotiations. For our Founders, slavery was a foul stain that interrupted and tainted an otherwise noble cause. Confronted with the dirty business, they tolerated the perversion, obscene to their ideals, in order to create a land where the "ideal", that all men are created equal, could be protected.

Faced with destruction from the world's most powerful military, our little nation was forced to swallow the bitter pill to join together the separate states in one righteous cause. To do otherwise would have guaranteed that America's Revolution would fail.

The United States' school system consistently reminds us of slavery's horrors; it burns into our children's minds images of lynching and of KKK rallies. It reminds us of Jim Crow and Dred Scott, and it does all this to our detriment. These stories are told over and over to demean our nation and to castigate us for our pride.

Little is taught about America's nobility or America's benevolence. Today reparations are demanded for a people sold into slavery by their own people in African nations, and these reparations are demanded from the "racist" white man. It matters not that over one-third of America's population are descendant from immigrants who came into the United States through Ellis Island between 1896 and 1924, long after slavery was abolished in the nation.

The Founders tolerated slavery in the South while those in the North loathed the practice because the issue was insurmountable when faced with the Revolutionary problems. Success in any endeavor requires a proper choice of battles. The slavery issue was reluctantly set aside to allow America's Founders to secure creation of this nation where eventually all men would be free.

Today Black Americans are among the most prosperous on earth and because of the difficult and distasteful compromises our Founders made; black opportunity in America is unparalleled in the world.

Who knows, because of the Founder's work, perhaps a black man will even become President of the United States one day!

Lincoln and Douglass: During the Civil War, black Union soldiers were paid a little more than half that their white counterparts were paid. They fought vigilantly as did the white soldiers, they were recognized for valor as were the white soldiers, and they died valiantly as white soldiers did, and yet the dichotomy.

Concerning this injustice, with President Abraham Lincoln in attendance, the former slave and abolitionist leader Frederick

Douglass made a spirited speech advocating that Negro men should join the Union Army.

He concluded his oratory with this:

"I hold that the Federal Government was never, in its essence, anything but an anti-slavery government. Abolish slavery tomorrow, and not a sentence or syllable of the Constitution need be altered. It was purposely so framed as to give no claim, no sanction to the claim of property in man. If in its origin slavery had any relation to the government, it was only as the scaffolding to the magnificent structure, to be removed as soon as the building was completed. There is in the Constitution no East, no West, no North, no South, no black, no white, no slave, no slaveholder, but all are citizens who are of American birth."

Douglass had a keen understanding and a keen appreciation for the thematic intent embodied in America's Constitution, and he knew that it was written never intending nor ever accepting the concept that slavery was a just or proper institution. Confronted by the obvious inequities of the times Douglass consistently worked to promote the American vision—that all men are created equal.

Lincoln's primary concern at onset of the Civil War had not been to free slaves, but to save the Union. In that regard he proclaimed,

"If I could save the Union, without freeing the slaves, I would do it. If I could do it by freeing some and leaving others alone, I would do that. What I do about slavery and the colored race, I do because I believe it would help to save the Union."

Whether or not Lincoln's statement reflected his own personal philosophy or whether it was presented with an understanding of political realities that ruled the day mattered not; Douglass understood Lincoln was much less concerned about the 2nd class status of Negro soldiers in the Union Army than he was and yet he still encouraged Negro Americans to support the Union cause and tolerate some temporary unfairness. Douglass knew the end objective of freedom would be the reward.

Even though Douglass differed with Lincoln they became good friends and the black soldier's efforts during the Civil War are considered essential to the Union's eventual victory.

If they concentrated on their differences rather than their shared goals their plight would not have been ameliorated.

Those striving for a Red State Coalition want the same thing as Douglass and his black soldiers:—freedom as promised by God in America's constitution.

Federalism—RIP

by RWR

One of the most compelling reasons we have to encourage the formation of a Red State Coalition is to reinvigorate the concept of Federalism, where government that is closest to the People is the government that most intimately and fairly rules the People.

The Articles of Confederation were in force from March 1, 1781, to June 21, 1788 and presented a loose framework for state cooperation. Due to our problems with Great Britain, the States feared the federal power and granted it little authority.

The system was unworkable, though, and without a strong central government with power to raise armies and levy taxes, the American Revolution nearly failed.

The United States Constitution was completed September 17, 1787 and began the ratification process. Governance under the Constitution began March 4, 1789. While this new law gave expanded powers to the central government, the Founders had trudged forward cautiously.

Powers were separated into three branches of government, the Executive would have broad rule where security of the nation was concerned, and able to perform military operations when necessary to protect the nation. The Executive had no lawmaking authority other than to approve or disapprove proposals made by Congress.

The Lawmaking branch was bifurcated between two houses, one of popular representation, the other of state representation and no proposed law could proceed without approval of both houses. More importantly, the legislative branch had only the powers enumerated in the Constitution. In other words, the Constitution proclaimed, "These are the only powers that are yours, Legislative Branch, what is not specified here, you cannot do."

In fact, in Article I, section 8, there were exactly eighteen specific enumerated powers allotted to Congress. What's not there they can't do—*legally*. But why let a mere ink-filled piece of parchment stop you when you are an important politician?

The third Branch of government, the Judicial, existed to make sure the other two didn't get out of line and it had no lawmaking powers.

The tenth amendment was proposed to insure powers not specifically delegated in the Constitution resided with the States and the People. Again, if it wasn't written the Judicial Branch was suppose to tell the legislators they couldn't do it.

Article V of the Constitution was included to provide mechanism for states and lawmakers to amend the Constitution *whenever two thirds of both Houses shall deem it necessary or…on the Application of the Legislatures of two thirds of the several States.*

The two thirds requirement set a high bar to insure laws would not be made "willy-nilly" at the whim of some whacked-out lawmaker, because if that was allowed, we might end up with an inconceivable and incomprehensible set of laws with over one thousand government agencies with varied authorities and enforcement powers, a tax code over 70,000 pages long, and an environment where every single citizen of America was not free, but a slave to the central power, and we would never want something like that!

Those founder guys were pretty smart, they kept us straight over a hundred years, but they could not possibly write law that would take into consideration the imagination and wickedness of our contemporary politician.

They did know that mankind had the power to destroy our Republic and our Constitution; James Madison prognosticated the possibility considering the clause, "general welfare".

"With respect to the two words 'general welfare', I have always regarded them as qualified by the detail of powers connected with them. To take them in a literal and unlimited sense would be a metamorphosis of the Constitution into a character which there is a host of proofs was not contemplated by its creators."

Federalism in the United States today is dead. There is no State sovereignty, and there is very little intimate connection between the States' inhabitants, its representatives, and the law which is thrust down upon them.

In fact, what we have today is worse than no Federalism. What we actually have is *anti-Federalism,* where our localities have no influence on local political policy, but far-flung entities in other states, along with Federal Government, promote policy we all must live under without consent.

Right now there is a movement to force the whole nation to abide by CO_2 emission standards set in California. Just the state in the union all others should try to emulate; with a deficit of 22 billion dollars!

Meanwhile, Texas has a robust and successful economy with a good business climate (one of the few states in the nation actually creating a couple of jobs) and politicians in Washington and Sacramento are conspiring to force Texas to adopt their job killing/economy killing regulations, because some moron at the EPA and Sheryl Crow said we are going to melt Greenland if these dumb Texans keep encouraging businesses with good tax policy and cheap electrical energy. And we wonder why Texans like guns.

Geraldo Rivera thinks the secessionists are whackos, but Sheryl Crow, she's a freaking genius!

Some of us remember learning in school that plants like to breathe CO_2 and humans like oxygen. Humans give off CO_2 when they breathe, and plants give off oxygen. I wonder if the government is going to put a cap on oxygen because when those humans keep breathing it they make too much CO_2?

Don't laugh, its coming.

Another important quality of Federalism that contributed to American prosperity was its inclination to encourage an improvement in law by seeing which States succeeded and which ones failed.

Going back to our CO_2 example, the citizens of Texas could take a good look over yonder and decide for themselves whether or not the emission caps and "carbon" taxes adopted in California would be advantageous for the good people of Texas.

They could even talk about it.

Californian: When are you Texans going to adopt a sound energy plan and tax your carbon emissions?

Texan: We have considered it, but we've seen y'all's economy hasn't fared so well under that policy.

Californian: If you don't do something quick, the earth is going to heat up, the polar ice caps are going to melt and the oceans are going to rise twenty feet.

Texan: It's already hot as hell here in Texas, one or two more degrees ain't gonna kill us, besides, the heat's good for Bar-B-Que.

Californian: If you stupid red-necks don't get off the dime all our businesses are going to leave the state because we can't compete; then we'll have a failing economy and global warming too!

Texan: Listen, we like to work here in Texas, we like cheap energy, and we like low taxes, now if you don't shut your trap I'm gonna put a cap in your ass!

This is the typical Federalist exchange which has served our country well, but now under our anti-Federalist system California has had recourse:

Californian: Yo, yo, yo, my brother Obama, listen here, these dumb Texan red-necks are jacking the environment and we can't compete with their business practices either.

Obama: Don't worry, I'll ram through another stimulus.

Californian: That won't do it, we need something that will destroy their economy like we have destroyed ours.

Obama: How about a national healthcare plan?

Californian: That will help, but we need something else.

Obama: O.K. I'll tell you what we are going to do. We'll make a treaty to limit carbon emissions that no one in the world will follow except for us, and those guys who make a lot of carbon will have to buy a carbon credit from those guys who don't make any, and since California is already doing that, Texas will now have the same problems you guys have.

Californian: That's good, that's good.

Obama: Also, I'll get my buddy Jeffrey Immelt at General Electric to setup a carbon credit brokerage company where he won't do nothing but trade carbon credits which really aren't anything at all and he'll make billions, and since GE's stock is in the tank, he'll really owe me.

You Texans better pay real close attention because the next thing Obama is going to do is limit your right to bear arms so he can then force you on to his carbon program without any resistance.

As I finish off this chapter, I'm thinking about Geraldo and his sanctimonious rant where gun-toting Texan secessionists are fringe lunatics, and where carbon credit Armageddonists are mainstream, and I can't help but think, is the world upside-down, or is it just me?

A Red State Coalition will reincarnate from the dead the dignified and honorable philosophy that men and women intimate with their communities should make the law that they must live under.

We can, *yes we can*, raise Federalism from the dead. This kind of *change* you can believe in.

Wealth   by RHL

Since so much of our nation's internecine bickering centers around the "unjustifiable" collection of wealth by our nation's upper classes, it seems reasonable to examine wealth, how it is formed, and how "redistributing" it will insure we all end up with less of it.

The theory (among those blessed with plenty of envy and not much ambition) that suggests wealth is a finite commodity in such sparse supply that it must be properly regulated cuts directly against those founding philosophies intimate to our original culture, and near and dear to those of us with great appreciation for and a strong desire to recapture—freedom.

This dispensation of wealth, being allowed to flourish and grow under those who create it or squandered by those of the political elite licensed with a popular vote mandate to confiscate it, is our most contentious divider motivating the formation of a Red State Coalition.

(Note: Citizens of Red State Coalition should be required to take an IQ test and a knowledge based test before being allowed to vote. We don't want to screw up the new Republic like we have screwed up the old one.)

"If a nation expects to be ignorant and free, in a state of civilization, it expects what never was and never will be." –Thomas Jefferson

When wealth is possessed by the individuals who developed it, its disposition will follow rules synergetic to its creation and pay no favor to the political wills intent on hijacking it, ergo, the creation of wealth will be encouraged. Conversely, the greater penalty we levy onto those who create wealth, the greater we will retard their wealth-creating activities.

The more wealth that we have in our society, the greater our standard of living available to all in society.

There is a misconception that wealth hoarded by upper classes is withheld from lower classes and therefore unavailable for use by the majority of society. Supposedly allowing the political power to redistribute this wealth, wealth will keep moving throughout our economy and more fairly distribute parts of this "finite" pie.

The real effect of this "redistribution" is to discourage the wealth producers from productive activity to protective activity. In other words, they will not work to build new wealth; they will work to protect the wealth that they already have.

If it were accurate that aggregate wealth causes depression and subjugates the working class, where is the model that shows that this is so?

What is required to start a new manufacturing plant that will employ people and provide opportunity for many in the working class? A building, machinery, raw materials and some sort of business plan might get you started, but without an aggregate of capital, these cannot be assembled.

More important than plans, machinery, and raw materials is the expertise essential to manage the business venture. And who might be better equipped to do the management and guarantee a successful outcome for the venture, the elected politician without any track record in wealth gathering activities, or the businessman who collected the capital to begin with?

Again, where do we really want wealth to congregate, with the entrepreneurs and intrepid businessmen who have honed their craft in the hard world of market demands, or with politicians whose only craft has been to get people to like them?

Wealth hoarded is useless, and unless Warren Buffet has 50 billion dollars stuffed under his mattress, wealth is not hoarded; it is invested and continues to circulate through society, providing benefit.

Even when wealth is not invested, when it is used for pleasure or for opulent and decadent consumption, it still gets back into the economy, providing jobs and opportunity for others.

If Warren Buffet purchases himself a new jet to fly around in, the action requires the creation of many jobs to manufacture, maintain, and to operate that jet. Would we prefer he use that jet and fly his butt off, or would we all be better off if he just stayed at home and read a book?

If he invests in companies requiring cash, or if he purchases stocks or bonds, all of that wealth is put back to work in society. He doesn't put this wealth back to work expecting that it is "finite" and will come back to him as it went; he expects his investment will create prosperity and bring him profit.

The assertion that government can grow an economy by borrowing, spending, or diverting wealth resources is ridiculous on its face. If politicians were so adept at such wealth management we wouldn't have such huge deficits and debt.

If Barney Frank and Ted Kennedy were adept at creating wealth, would they be working in government for a $200,000.00 a year salary, or would they be working in private industry like Warren Buffet making 50 million dollars a year?

Would we prefer that guys like Warren Buffet be allowed to control the wealth they have developed or would we prefer that job stay under purview of Barney Frank and Ted Kennedy?

If you said Warren Buffet, you'll probably be a new citizen in the Red State Coalition!

There is a fallacy, promoted by some adverse to our capitalist heritage, that says the Great Depression was created due to an unequal distribution of wealth. This is typical political rancor great on rhetoric based without fact and designed only to encourage groups already predisposed to envy.

It is as if to say, because your neighbor has three big screen TVs, two new SUV's and a boat, while you only have an old beat up Ford Pinto, this "unfair" distribution will cause society to experience depression. If only the selfish neighbor would give you a big screen and one SUV, all would be well.

If we could just share the wealth around as Barack Obama sermonized to "Joe the Plumber," ostensibly all of our economic problems would be avoided.

Instead of considering this idiocy, let's consider where wealth exists and how it is created.

Africa produces nearly 50 percent of the world's diamonds, chromium, and platinum and has greater oil reserves than all of North America, yet its inhabitants are among the poorest on the planet.

Israel is one country with some six million Jews on a plot of land about as big as Vermont with few natural resources. Surrounded by 450 million Arabs, all wishing for Israel's destruction, the little country boasts the region's most powerful military, and person for person its most active and vibrant economy.

If wealth were defined by the possession of natural resources, Africa would be rich and Israel poor.

We might consider that wealth is composed by controlling labor, because without labor goods and services cannot be built. This is the ideological assertion claimed by worker's unions, but if wealth was acquired by subjugating labor then the antebellum south should have dominated the north and yet it was precisely because of this reliance on subjugated labor instead of intellectual creativity that their plight was doomed.

If labor by itself created wealth, all the workers of the nation could leave their "despotic" masters and combine their resources to become wealthy. Now that the UAW owns substantial shares of General Motors and Chrysler, they ought to be the most successful car companies on the planet!

Labor and raw materials are useless commodities without intellectual input, and with intellectual input valueless resources can gain worth.

The next time you go to work you might consider thanking your company for making you worth something!

Examine the nations around the world with the most prosperity and it is clear that the nations which best protect economic freedom possess the most wealth; because wealth is not built by resources, it is built by *minds*. Minds will not flourish under the tyranny where intellectual efforts are stifled by the politician's confiscatory sword.

The more our politicians penalize our economic freedom, the more they discourage our intellectual outputs and limit our nation's wealth.

Our Red State Coalition must be dedicated to economic freedom if it expects to encourage intellectual output to generate wealth and therefore prosperity.

When our little group debated what to keep and what to cut from this manuscript, this chapter was top of the chopping block because about half of our crew felt it fell outside the general theme of the book which we understood to be American prosperity in relationship to founding principles, and the need for a new nation dedicated to restoring prosperity and those principles.

The chapter stayed in because those wanting to keep it won the day by arguing that wealth is the engine of prosperity and any attempt to control it by the political power most definitely limits wealth and limits prosperity, and no country, including our Red State Coalition can prosper without a robust and creative wealth generating populace.

Property <small>by JKP</small>

*Among the natural rights of the Colonists are these First a Right to Life; Secondly to Liberty; thirdly to **Property**; together with the Right to support and defend them in the best manner they can—Those are evident Branches of, rather than deductions from the Duty of Self Preservation, commonly called the first law of Nature. -Resolutions of Boston, 1772*

Members of our political elite don't like Natural Law because it contains everything required by individuals to resist despotic government. Natural Law demands that certain freedoms are just not within authority of any government power. The right to breathe, to eat, to protect oneself and one's property are all humans rights given to mankind by God. While corrupt government dogma asks that individuals look to it for personal preservation, God's law demands that the individual is the best defender of self-evident freedoms.

And revisionists want you to believe the right to bear arms is a "collective" right.

From Virginia's Declaration of Rights, adopted unanimously by the Virginia Convention of Delegates on June 12, 1776:

A declaration of rights made by the representatives of the good people of Virginia, assembled in full and free convention; which rights do pertain to them and their posterity, as the basis and foundation of government.

*SECTION I. That all men are by nature equally free and independent and have certain inherent rights, of which, when they enter into a state of society, they cannot, by any compact, deprive or divest their posterity; namely, the enjoyment of life and liberty, with the means of acquiring and possessing **property**, and pursuing and obtaining happiness and safety.*

Any in-depth study of philosophy and thought attributable to the founding generation consistently reveals their dedication to the idea that *property* was an inalienable right.

There is even speculation that Jefferson broke with the standard of the day in substituting "the pursuit of happiness" for "property" when drafting the Declaration of Independence, not to broaden its appeal, but to preemptively castigate the institution of slavery where slaves were considered "property" of their masters, which was completely incompatible with the spirit of the Declaration and its intent.

Beyond the founding era, property was still lauded important and sacred:

"Property is the fruit of labor...property is desirable...is a positive good in the world. That some should be rich shows that others may become rich, and hence is just encouragement to industry and enterprise. Let not him who is houseless pull down the house of another; but let him labor diligently and build one for himself, thus by example assuring that his own shall be safe from violence when built." -Abraham Lincoln

Perhaps the best declaration that mankind must be allowed *the fruits of his labor* in a moral and just society comes from Jefferson:

"To take from one because it is thought that his own industry and that of his father's has acquired too much, in order to spare to others, who, or whose fathers, have not exercised equal industry and skill, is to violate arbitrarily the first principle of association—the guarantee to every one of a free exercise of his industry and the fruits acquired by it." -Thomas Jefferson

It is almost pointless to argue moral principle in today's American society where moral hazard has been hijacked by politicians to ensure bad or irresponsible behavior will be held to no account and those who have attained some property are forced to cover all costs required by those who haven't.

Our current system has actually incentivized doing nothing. If you do something and acquire property you owe it to the government. If you do nothing and acquire nothing, the government will give you something.

I wonder what Geraldo thinks about that? Anybody who works in this system would have to be a "fringe" whack job *not* to desire secession.

An individual's property is not a collection of inanimate objects, nor is it materialistic evidence of society's decadent and selfish culture; property is the just reflection of an individual's hard work and effort. If government can arbitrarily take a person's property, then government is master and individual is slave.

For the average American worker, doing less is the only recourse available to reduce financial "obligations" demanded by government. This causes lower tax revenues to government, which in turn increases its demands on producers, encouraging them to do even less.

The more government promotes confiscatory policy on citizen property, the more citizens will endeavor *not* to create or obtain property of value.

Meanwhile, those big business leaders and elites in government will exempt themselves and/or subsidize themselves with preferential tax credits and incentives that the average citizen will never have access to.

"The trouble with socialism is that eventually you run out of other people's money." -Margaret Thatcher

Life   by KMP

When in the Course of human events, it becomes necessary for one people to dissolve the political bands which have connected them with another, and to assume among the powers of the earth, the separate and equal station to which the Laws of Nature and of Nature's God entitle them, a decent respect to the opinions of mankind requires that they should declare the causes which impel them to the separation.

We hold these truths to be self-evident, that all men are created equal, that they are endowed by their Creator with certain unalienable Rights, that among these are Life, Liberty and the pursuit of Happiness. —That…

When describing unalienable rights, the Declaration of Independence lists life first, liberty second, and the pursuit of happiness, third.

The Founders were extensively influenced by Free Masons, by Cicero, and an historic record that could reveal few nations successfully ruled by self-determination.

What the Founders wanted to create was a "New Order for the Ages". To do it they had to place that most treasured and unalienable right recognized not only by God, but by mankind's natural reason at a pinnacle point to which all other important yet lesser rights would yield.

Life was listed first in the Declaration because if ever there would be conflict between unalienable rights the latter would yield to the former.

What makes a nation great, what gives it fortitude and character is the moral fiber from which it is constructed. Without protecting life, that foundation is undermined.

It is quite peculiar that our Blue camp buddies, who portray themselves guardian of the vulnerable and protector of the downtrodden would actively and ferociously fight any of our state's attempts to regulate or prevent the practice of abortion.

In fact, they sling vituperative arrows at the pro-life crowd, only for suggesting that the standard for permissible abortion be set any higher than a mother's whim.

If the unborn are not the most vulnerable and downtrodden among us I wonder who is.

What kind of society evolves when God's most precious gift is tossed about with impertinent disregard?

China under Mao, and Russia under Stalin come to mind.

In fact, Russia was the first nation on earth to legalize abortion and under Lenin, Russia purged religion from its culture. Russia's Revolutionary leaders surmised, if they could get their people to throw aside God and kill babies, they could get them to do anything.

It probably won't surprise the reader, even though Russia has adopted a flat tax structure which relieved much of it's revenue problem, the nation's corruption is still some of the worst among industrialized nations.

The incidence of AIDS in Russia is three times what it is in the U.S.

Their murder rate is five time ours.

When life is cheap, so is everything else.

If Blue Campers want to encourage and expand this culture, fine, but those of us who revere Life need our own country—A Red State Coalition.

God by LEW

On August 26, 1776, George Washington led his troops in the first major battle of the Revolutionary War. The Continental Army had successfully driven the British from Boston five months earlier with hardly a shot. Washington had the advantage of high ground then, but this battle would not be so defined.

Over one hundred British ships patrolled the New York Bay and over thirty thousand British troops were mustered on Staten Island. Washington had nineteen thousand troops in all of New York, and no Navy.

Venturing to avoid military action, General Howe, commander of British forces, sent his adjutant, Colonel James Patterson, to negotiate with Washington. Patterson told Washington that if his army laid down arms, General Howe had powers to grant pardons.

Washington replied, "Those who have committed no fault want no pardon."

The battle of New York was a disaster for Washington, American deaths were three times that suffered by the British, and one thousand Americans were taken prisoner. Washington was out flanked and out maneuvered and found his army surrounded with the East River at his back.

If General Howe pressed the fight here, Washington would have been defeated and the Revolution would have been over.

For two days, Washington held the ground at Brooklyn Heights, but his Generals recommended retreat across the East River to Manhattan.

The crossing was one mile and steady wind from the North had prevented British ships from sailing up the Bay to block the escape route.

On August 29, at 11:00 in the evening, Washington's army began evacuating Brooklyn Heights across the East River. Some of the troops maintained campfires to distract the British. Throughout the night the army quietly made the crossing, fearful they could not complete the effort by daybreak.

As day broke, a heavy fog settled in concealing the American's retreat. Suspicious of little activity, British scouts began to search the area sounding alarms, as Washington, the last man to evacuate Brooklyn stepped on the last boat.

By nine in the morning all nine thousand of Washington's men rested safely on Manhattan Island.

Washington felt the hand of Providence had shielded his army and he felt the American struggle was a just one blessed by God. This belief drove Washington to overcome unfathomable obstacles to come.

The fortitude, determination and sanguine faith possessed by America's Founders were exceptional and unusual. There was no reason to expect that America could stand up to the world's most powerful and best-trained military, yet it did. American's believed they could, not because their military was superior but because their cause was superior. Their cause was blessed by God.

Why didn't General Howe prosecute the battle when he had the upper hand to finish off the Americans?

Why did the wind blow stubbornly southward preventing the British Navy from cutting off Washington's escape route?

Why did the fog roll in that early morning just in time to cloak the American retreat?

The warm shield of God, or just coincidence?

On the back of the one dollar bill is the Great Seal of the United States. On the circle to the right (the front of the seal) thirteen stars for our original colonies adorn space just above the eagle's head which is characteristically looking to the right toward the olive branch held in its right talon signifying America's desire for peace. In the eagle's left talon are arrows reminding all that peace exists only through strength. Covering the eagle's chest is a shield of red, white, and blue, and above the eagle a ribbon embossed, "E PLURIBUS UNUM".

Centered in the left circle (the back of the Great Seal) sits an unfinished pyramid with roman numerals etched into the base, "MDCCLXXVI" (1776). Below the embossed ribbon reads, NOVUS ORDO SECLORUM", which translates, "a new order of the ages." Thirteen levels of stone are used to construct the pyramid, one level for each colony, but the pyramid is cut short to show America is a work in progress. Above the pyramid is the all seeing eye of providence watching over America and above this the motto, "ANNUIT COEPTIS," meaning, "He favors our undertakings."

While the United States Supreme Court consistently hands down rulings hostile to "God" in our schools and our public places, the Supreme Court building is itself adorned with many reverences to God. The Ten Commandments are inscribed in more than one location in or on the building and Moses stands holding the tablets above the building's main entrance.

While our generation looks to the Founder's with admiration and wonder, so too did they look to their forefathers of history:

"True law is right reason in agreement with Nature...it is of universal application, unchanging and everlasting.... we need not look outside ourselves for an expounder or interpreter of it. And there will not be different laws at Rome and at Athens, or different laws now and in the future, but one eternal and unchangeable law will be valid for all nations and for all times, and there will be one master and one rule, that is, God, over us all, for He is the author of this law, its promulgator, and its enforcing judge." -Cicero

Cicero is a good guy to quote when Blue Campers start going off unhinged in support of that "living Constitution" nonsense.

Understanding how God's law and God's guidance have been instrumental in the creation and development of our country, how can we survive and prosper by throwing aside everything that has defined us?

While the United States may try, a Red State Coalition of Americans will not.

"The God who gave us life gave us liberty at the same time; the hand of force may destroy, but cannot disjoin them." -Thomas Jefferson

Amendment Number Two by DRW

It has been said, "Without the 2nd Amendment, the rest are basically worthless."

Our politicians adeptly and dishonestly argue about the dangers inherent in a society that possesses guns. "We need to save the children," but only from deaths resulting from guns, not from the other much more prevalent and common causes. All the child deaths by handguns each year don't add up to the deaths occurring from falling down stairs, yet there is no political effort to abolish stairs. And where is the effort to abolish swimming pools and trampolines?

Stairs are no threat to the parasites that populate Washington DC, and therefore there is no reason to eliminate them.

Mayor Michael Bloomberg of New York recently lamented that a concealed carry bill favored by portions of Congress would allow "criminals" to carry concealed weapons freely—Mayor Bloomberg is a flat-out liar. Just try and get a concealed carry permit and see what you need to go through to get it.

It's not that the world is so dangerous that everybody needs a gun in their pocket, or that possession absolutely guarantees safety, but there were two important reasons the Founders insured we would have the right to bear arms.

Suffering under the British, they wanted to ensure dictatorial rule would be met with armed opposition, but they also recognized that self-preservation is an inalienable right not within government's authority to withhold from mankind.

This revelation follows the intuitive reasoning of Natural Law, and only becomes a point of contention when humanistic thought is manipulated to subjugate our faith and our rights for political advantage.

Ultimately, the Founders provided the right to bear arms to ensure the government power remained in its rightful place, subordinate to the people.

The despotic character of Britain over the colonies could not have been overcome without access to arms, and today's despotic characters in government will not be controlled without maintaining an access to arms.

The 2nd Amendment is the one that ensures all the others remain in their rightful place accessible to the People.

We must remember every "sensible" proposal discussed by bureaucrats, concerning gun control, is intended in preserving bureaucratic power not in protecting the people. In support of that end, government officials will use propaganda in the form of official government memorandum where the intended goal is to move citizens to accept assaults on their freedom that are ostensibly perpetrated on their behalf.

On April 14 2009, the Department of Homeland Security under Janet Napolitano released a memo entitled, *Rightwing Extremism: Current Economic and Political Climate Fueling Resurgence in Radicalization and Recruitment.*

Here are some of the best bits from that memo,

"The DHS/Office of Intelligence and Analysis (I&A) has no specific information that domestic rightwing terrorists are currently planning acts of violence, but rightwing extremists may be gaining new recruits by playing on their fears about several emergent issues. The economic downturn and the election of the first African American president present unique drivers for rightwing radicalization and recruitment."

Of course it is not the *First African American president which causes a unique driver for rightwing radicalization and recruitment*, it is this President's propensity to act like a dictator and take away America's right to bear arms which does it.

"Many rightwing extremist groups perceive recent gun control legislation as a threat to their right to bear arms…"

>Well how else would we expect them to perceive it?

"…and in response have increased weapons and ammunition stockpiling, as well as renewed participation in paramilitary training exercises. "

>Just as our Founding Fathers would have expected.

"Such activity, combined with a heightened level of extremist paranoia, has the potential to facilitate criminal activity and violence."

>That last bit should have said, "Such activity has the potential to keep the government within its expected sphere of authority!"

"Rightwing extremists are harnessing this historical election as a recruitment tool. Many rightwing extremists are antagonistic toward the new presidential administration and its perceived stance on a range of issues, including immigration and citizenship, the expansion of social programs to minorities, and restrictions on firearms ownership and use. Rightwing extremists are increasingly galvanized by these concerns and leverage them as drivers for recruitment. From the 2008 election timeframe to the present, rightwing extremists have capitalized on related racial and political prejudices in expanded propaganda campaigns, thereby reaching out to a wider audience of potential sympathizers."

>How many of you reading this book, *are antagonistic toward the new presidential administration and its perceived stance on a range of issues, including immigration and citizenship, the expansion of social programs, and restrictions on firearms ownership and use?*

"The willingness of a small percentage of military personnel to join extremist groups during the 1990s because they were disgruntled, disillusioned, or suffering from the psychological effects of war is being replicated today."

— (U) After Operation Desert Shield/Storm in 1990-1991, some returning military veterans—including Timothy McVeigh—joined or associated with rightwing extremist groups.

Of course there is also no mention of the *small percentage of military personnel* who go home and hack up their whole family with a butcher knife, but that happens too!

This memorandum used the term rightwing extremist 39 times and not once did it ever mention any danger to freedom due to our "leftwing" extremists.

That, of course, is silly because the leftwing extremists all work for the government and they are responsible for writing this stupid memo.

No warning was made in regard to the leftwing extremist organization, *Earth First*, which is likely to burn down more car dealerships this year if Obama doesn't get his cap and trade bill passed.

If you have guns and ammo you're going to be on the government's watch list, and if you undertake training to become proficient with your arms and listen to talk radio, you're public enemy number one.

This memo was so full of ridiculous leftist propaganda we could have just listed the whole thing passage by passage and called it an "Obama" campaign speech.

The writers of this book debated this official government correspondence and concluded we are all very likely *rightwing extremists*, and we have jobs and kids and even little dogs; some of us served proudly in the United States Military and came back home without shooting even one single person.

If you are sympathetic to the idea that our government should be more active in regulating and registering arms in America here is a recap:

The Soviet Union instituted gun controls in 1929, and between 1929 and 1959 it killed over 20 million political dissidents.

China instituted gun controls in 1935 and by 1952 it had killed more than 20 million political dissidents.

Germany had fairly strict gun control laws; implemented by the Weimar Republic in 1919. In 1938 the Nazi regime actually reduced gun control restrictions on all groups except for one. That group was completely forbidden to possess arms.

Hmmm, I wonder what happened to them?

These kinds of atrocities will never be allowed in a Red State Coalition, but they might be in the United States.

Accomplishment, Honor and Virtue by GLB

America's Founders knew that the average citizen, busy providing for family and self, would not be well enough engaged and knowledgeable of the political issues of the day to make the best decisions regarding their own rule. Thus, America's Republic was designed so that those possessed with the greatest "accomplishment, honor, and virtue" would rise to become our nation's representatives.

A moral and religious people would always select those candidates of accomplishment with the greatest honor and virtue, and these are the candidates who would most likely make the decisions that would safeguard America and preserve our rights and our liberties.

Accomplishment reveals an individual's capacity for succeeding in our system and suggests probable competence in the job he must perform. Honorable men would definitively work on the public's behalf, whether or not anyone was watching over them, and virtue in our leaders would provide good example for society to emulate.

Born out of religious persecution, the American colonial movement attracted people from all over Europe aspiring to be free and able to worship as they saw fit. This heritage anchored the colonies firmly to God and provided an atmosphere ripe to indulge and experiment with self-rule. This foundation would insure that only those of accomplishment, of honor, and of virtue would rise to high office.

The United States has evolved far away from that origin where all of our people were deferent to God and his Natural Law and many feel no slight or dismay that our Godly underpinnings have been stripped away.

While serving as diplomat in Paris with Thomas Jefferson and Benjamin Franklin, John Adams, quite perturbed with the French culture lamented, "What can be expected from 500,000 atheists?" His eerie rumination would be answered in the schizophrenic and gruesome French Revolution that starkly contrasted America's Revolution which was fought with intent and purpose.

Considering a future without God in culture, John Adams noted, "Our Constitution was written for a moral and religious people and it is wholly inadequate for any other."

The Congress of the United States is comprised of representatives from all fifty states. There are about five hundred people to represent some 300 million. If there was one representative for every 30,000 citizens as originally chartered by America's Founders, today members of Congress would number 10,000. Most American's feel little or no connection to their elected representatives, and why should they? Who really believes congressional representatives are really out to serve anyone other than themselves?

Devoid the qualities of accomplishment, honor and virtue, we find today's politicians happy to give themselves pay raises and cost of living adjustments without voter approval.

What they pay themselves is miniscule, however, compared to what they spend on "our" behalf, and how they use tax incentives to curry favor with those who might repay them with cushy jobs or insider stock information.

One might ask, how is it a guy like Al Gore leaves office as Vice President with a net worth of one or two million dollars and within a few years amasses a fortune north of 100 million dollars? Never mind that he was mercilessly chastised by *Fortune Magazine* for having financial acumen "not worth a bucket of warm spit!"

I suppose his stint as VP is only coincidental to his massive increase in personal wealth? While Gore and other politicians see their personal wealth skyrocket, the United States has only gone much deeper into debt.

Without accomplishment, honor and virtue held in abundant amounts by our elected officials, not only will our country become bankrupt financially, we will become bankrupt morally and spiritually.

The United States is not stopping or slowing its march toward secular government or secular schools and is, in fact, insisting that secular thought transcend all American thought. It is attacking our Christian roots and perverting the language to suggest that moral thought is "judgmental" and "close-minded" thought.

We have become a nation where accomplishment, honor and virtue are interpreted to be arrogant qualities worthy ridicule. Often, today's politicians have no accomplishment, honor or virtue, and their only aspiration as elected officials is to take whatever they can get.

A Red State Coalition must admire the precepts of accomplishment, honor and virtue. Without them prosperity for all cannot flourish.

Constitutional Contortionists by RHL

If growing wheat on your own land for your own consumption affects interstate commerce, is it not true that repairing your own automobile in your own driveway has a likewise effect? Following this train of thought, what action can a United States citizen take which does not affect interstate commerce?

The concept that United States Constitutional government is one of limited powers has been completely obliterated by our Supreme Court. Today, the Constitution says whatever our politicians and Supreme Court say it says whenever they decide to say it.

The idea that a lowly citizen of the United States might read the Founding documents and determine its meaning is pointless because our politicians have discerned that our Constitution must be viewed as a "living document".

"Living" meaning that the words in the documents mean something different today than what they meant when they were written.

For all intents and purposes we have no Constitution, we have a political oligarchy, and "the people" are their subjects. They own us. Those of us vying for the formation of a Red State Coalition do so because we believe that no man should be another man's property or be enslaved to another man's his will.

Many point to the 1942 decision in **Wickard v. Filburn,** where Congress could regulate what a private citizen could do on his own land for his own private consumption as a watershed moment in our evolution toward oligarchy, but Theodore Roosevelt with his progressive programs, Woodrow Wilson's policies and creation of the Federal Reserve, and FDR's far-reaching New Deal programs all contributed to this deterioration of American freedom and transfer of power to the political elite.

Today in fact, the law handed down to citizens of the United States has virtually nothing to do with what the Constitution says, but everything to do with what those who sit on the Supreme Court *say* it says.

Law is not supposed to be confusing and it is not suppose to be controversial either. Law is written to allow mankind an environment where everyone has equal opportunity on a level playing field. The law is conceived so that, *"A wise old woman and a wise old man would eventually reach the same conclusion in a case",* as stated by Supreme Court Justice Sandra Day O'Connor. In practice this may not always be the case, but as a general concept we can consider O'Connor's sentiments the prudent ideal to aim for.

In contrast, our latest nominee to the Supreme Court, Sonia Sotomayor, has opined, *"I would hope that a wise Latina woman with the richness of her experiences would more often than not reach a better conclusion than a white male who hasn't lived that life."*

Reach a better conclusion for whom?

If you are a white firefighter named Frank Ricci working for the city of New Haven and you pass a rigorous advancement exam when none of your Black coworkers do, *the richness of her experience* just might cause you to lose your promotion.

There is a reason Lady Justice is blindfolded when ascertaining proper balance for the scales in her left hand, and it is not so that she will adjudicate *with the richness of her experience* and discount the law.

When the Founders demarcated the three branches of government, they expected that the Judiciary would be the most noble and expected it to slow the other two down. Today that branch of government leads the other two and *legislates* itself.

In accordance with Article V, the Constitution of the United States can be amended, yet this has only occurred 27 times. As the Founders intended, the Constitution is difficult to amend, and this puts roadblocks in front of activist judges and politicians who want to increase their own powers and limit citizen freedoms.

To really understand how precarious and unpredictable our law has become we need only to review some recent and infamous Supreme Court decisions:

Kelo v. City of New London—The Court decided the City of New London could condemn private property owned by one private individual and sell it to another private individual if the second individual would develop it in such a way as to bring more tax revenue into the city.

McCreary County v. ACLU of Kentucky—The Court decided a monument erected at a Kentucky courthouse which displayed the Ten Commandments was unconstitutional.

District of Columbia v. Heller—The Court decided Washington DC's law preventing a private citizen from possessing a handgun in his own home was unconstitutional.

Bush v. Gore—The Court decided that all recounts must cease and the election must be certified in accordance with Florida law. (The Court took this action after two Florida recounts proclaimed George Bush to have won both times, whereby Al Gore submitted an arbitrary request to recount only those counties that tended to overwhelmingly vote for Democratic candidates.)

Boumediene v. Bush—The Court ruled that enemy combatants of war maintained habeas corpus rights guaranteed to our citizens in the Constitution.

These are pretty foundational cases:

Do we have the right to bear arms?

Are we entitled to our own private property?

Can public officials encourage an embrace of God, or only discourage such embrace?

Who will be our next president?

Do foreign fighters against us get Constitutional protections or are they treated like enemy combatants?

In each of these cases the Supreme Court was split five to four. These laws set precedent that the American people will have to tolerate for many years and yet, *wise old women and wise old men have reached completely different conclusions in these cases* and only by the prerogative of one single person on the United States Supreme Court.

In matters of conscience, the law of majority has no place. -Mahatma Gandhi

The whole point of Constitutional Law is to set down standards that will protect fundamental rights of citizens that even the majority cannot overrule. If words are interpreted to be so arbitrary, *that wise old women and wise old men* cannot discern them then we have no law, we have dictatorship where those in government prescribe what we can say, what we can do and how we will live.

The Supreme Court of a Red State Coalition must be dedicated to the concept that our Constitutional Law has the authority to restrain the political will of mere men and women in elected office, and maintain government in its rightful place: **servant to the people.**

Palin-ology by SMC

A quick review of Sarah Palin's candidacy for Vice President illuminates emphatically how divided our nation is and how attempting to maintain our union is not only impossible, it is foolish.

Here is a woman who went into politics because she didn't like the way her little town was being run, became its mayor and garnered excellent approval ratings from her townspeople. Following up on this success she ran for governor of her state challenging the established politicians in her *own* party accusing them of corruption and favoritism. She won that election and up until her run with John McCain, enjoyed the best popularity rating of any governor in the nation.

Sarah Palin epitomizes Middle America. She is a happy Christian mother of five children married to a blue-collar guy who works in the oil fields of Alaska's North Slope. When the child of her last pregnancy was confirmed to have Down syndrome she proceeded to term never considering abortion. She helps her husband run a small seasonal fishing business, and she hunts moose. She is what Washington elites hate most; bright and successful by her own merit

The Blue Camp despises this woman so intently that even after she resigned as governor of Alaska to get out of the limelight, the assaults on her and her family were only ratcheted up.

We have to wonder what it is that causes such deep seated hatred.

She was accused of being stupid, a slut, ditzy, trailer trash, etc. You would think if she was as dumb as portrayed she would be the Blue Camp's dream candidate—so easy to defeat, and yet the onslaught continued, even after her resignation from politics.

Meanwhile, those in Middle America disconnected from the snooty and arrogant community within academia thought she was terrific. She was folksy, honest, and wore the home spun Christian values that originally defined America, proudly for all to see.

It didn't really bother us that Charlie Gibson ambushed her with an esoteric question about *Bush Doctrine*, or that Katie Couric edited her interview with the governor to make her look dumb. And while we probably wished she knew a little bit more about Supreme Court cases, on the most important things she was right on. On freedom, on liberty, on life, and on hard work, she had the right positions.

Some of her cameo responses were a little schizophrenic and meandering, but compared to Barack Obama, who couldn't get through a paragraph without about thirty "dah"s if off teleprompter, her performance wasn't so bad for someone thrust into the national limelight.

While State controlled media outlets (ABC, NBC, CBS) asserted that *"Barack Obama just might be the smartest man to ever inhabit the presidency"*, Sarah Palin was portrayed even dumber than George Bush or Ronald Reagan, two of the dumbest presidents ever to inhabit the White House, according to the same media elitists.

We take exception to the silly assertion that Barack Obama is the *"brightest man"* ever to make it to the White House, but even if it were true, what good is high intellect if it is prostituted to empower government and enslave the People. We would rather have a dim bulb with good values as president than a genius determined to *"fundamentally change America"* as Barack Obama promised before taking office.

What if you don't want to fundamentally change America? What if you like the idea that we have freedom of speech, freedom of religion, right to bear arms, the right to choose our own health care providers, and the right to prosper by our own efforts?

Fundamentally changing America means that these rights are not unalienable; it means these rights will be dispersed by government as mortal men see fit. *Fundamentally changing America* means the People will not answer or be accountable to God; they will be accountable to the elected officials who populate Washington DC.

Sarah Palin is a microcosm of what *is* the United States today. The divisions about her are so stark and so irreconcilable, how in good conscience can we expect or why would we even desire that this union be maintained? With such divisive culture and so much internecine hatred, what do we expect to accomplish by not securing a Red State Coalition separate from the United States where those who worship God can continue to do so and where those who would rather worship the leaders of the State can have their way?

The General United Electric States of America by GLB

When my buddies and I got together to talk before Obama's election and inauguration, we mourned the impending disaster. Both Obama and McCain demonstrated a predisposition to be even more inclined to blow money than Bush, and we felt either one would cause a mess. In our wildest imagination we could not have dreamed up the nightmare that has taken place.

George Bush presided over the greatest increase in the nation's deficit in history (although he did have 9/11 to contend with since the Clinton administration destroyed the intelligence services), but Obama increased it four-fold in only six months.

Who in their right mind would believe you if you said, "Six months after the next president is inaugurated unemployment is going to be ten percent and Chrysler, GM, and all of our biggest banks are going to be bankrupt, the largest insurance company, AIG, will accept $150 billion in bailout funds and then give hundreds of millions in bonuses to their executives, but Fannie Mae and Freddie Mac, whose policies destroyed the real estate market, will require even more bailout money and they will reward their executives with even greater bonuses than AIG"?

The one bank that didn't get into any trouble, Bank of America, was in excellent financial shape because its executives steered clear of the secondary mortgage market recognizing it was a house of cards. Why then did it agree to buy Merrill Lynch which was headed for the same fate as all the other financial institutions due to its holdings in bad mortgage debt?

Coming under fire for pressuring Bank of America's CEO, Ken Lewis, Secretary of the Treasury Hank Paulson told Congress, *"Reneging on a promise to purchase Merrill Lynch would show a colossal lack of judgment and under such circumstance the Federal Reserve would be justified in removing management at the bank."*

Furthermore, Paulson pressed, *"By referring to the Federal Reserve's supervisory powers, I intended to deliver a strong message reinforcing the view that had been consistently expressed by the Federal Reserve, as Bank of America's regulator, and shared by the Treasury, that it would be unthinkable for Bank of America to take this destructive action for which there was no reasonable legal basis and which would show a lack of judgment."*

One has to wonder, to what destructive action was Paulson referring? As CEO of Bank of America, Ken Lewis is first answerable to his stockholders, not the government, but evidently that is not so in the General United Electric States of America, where the division between government and business has been completely eliminated.

In Paulson's view, private enterprise and Ken Lewis are answerable to the government and not recognizing this responsibility illustrates a *"colossal lack of judgment."*

You might disagree if you held Bank of America stock in September 2008 where it was valued at about thirty-five bucks a share. By March 2009 it was barely above three dollars. That is a loss in value of nearly 90 percent, and a public official threatening punitive action on a private party managing a private enterprise on behalf of private citizens perpetrated this fiasco.

Some call this fascism! To see where countries that experience this sort of government construction end up you might review the history of Germany under Hitler, Spain under Franco, or Italy under Mussolini.

Just when we thought things could not get any worse the president has forcefully promoted and endorsed a cap and trade tax scheme where conveniently, General Electric, a major campaign contributor, has positioned itself to profit significantly by brokering the carbon emission credits which will be mandatory under the cap and trade program.

General Electric won't be making anything or developing any new technologies; they are just the government endorsed entity that will trade "credits" when the government arbitrarily decides that some of us produce too much carbon dioxide and will have to buy "carbon credits" to "offset" our unauthorized CO_2 production.

In other words, we will be taxed and the money won't go to the government, it will go to General Electric, and this is so when Obama gets out of office he can get a real nice paying job after having to live off a mediocre government salary all this time.

This blending of big business and government has characterized the evolution of fascism in the past and it has always been followed by an infringement on citizen rights.

We would say Obama is kind of like Hitler but then people would call us crazy.

In a Red State Coalition, we will be dedicated to the kind of environment where freedom and capitalism are hostile to this fascist evolution.

I...American   by PVJ

"In the first place, we should insist that if the immigrant who comes here in good faith becomes an American and assimilates himself to us, he shall be treated on an exact equality with everyone else, for it is an outrage to discriminate against any such man because of creed, or birthplace, or origin. But, this is predicated upon the man's becoming in very fact an American, and nothing but an American. There can be no divided allegiance here. Any man who says he is an American, but something else also, isn't an American at all. We have room for but one flag, the American flag ... and this excludes the red flag, which symbolizes all wars against liberty and civilization, just as much as it excludes any foreign flag of a nation to which we are hostile. We have room for but one language here, and that is the English language. And we have room for but one sole loyalty, and that is a loyalty to the American people."

Theodore Roosevelt 1907

    Theodore Roosevelt did plenty wrong that got us down the progressive road, but on immigration and multi-culturalism the old Rough Rider was pretty much on point.
    No nation survives without loyalty to common cause, common culture, and common man.
    Those of us concerned that North America's evolution will see a United States broken into two nations are only so decided because it is clear that citizens of the current United States are not loyal to a common cause and culture. Moreover, we do not find brotherhood in our citizenship, we find distrust.
    The cultural qualities that define Americans are qualities that have always set us apart from other nations.
    Americans historically have been an unruly lot, distrusting of authority, self-sufficient, and adamant about personal freedoms.
    Americans don't want special favors for themselves. Americans want freedom and liberty for all. They want the same opportunities for themselves and their countrymen. Americans want to see all people prosper, and all Americans to have the same opportunities and possibilities. Whether they are Hispanic immigrants who want to be Americans or Asian immigrants who

want to be Americans or Black or White or Red or Green citizens who are already Americans, what Americans want is universal prosperity which comes through diligent hard work, some prayer, a little luck, and a lot of faith.

Americans don't want special regulations that pit one group against another and government pronouncements that encourage distrust of fellow citizens. Americans don't want arbitrary rules that penalize one faction or favor another because one or the other is politically connected. Americans don't want to promote an immoral agenda, and this puts them at odds with members of the Blue Camp who are much more interested in personal power than moral policy.

To maintain a nation's culture, orderly and consistent immigration policies must be adhered to assimilate and absorb one people into another.

Today we don't have an America with Hispanics, and Whites and Blacks; we have Black Americans, and White Americans and Hispanic Americans. When we identify ourselves as Black or White or Asian or Hispanic first and American second, what kind of nation can we expect to have?

Some of the authors in our group are grandchildren of those who came through Ellis Island. We are Italian, German, Spanish and Greek, and we all have one thing in common, none of us speak the language of our grandparent's homeland.

We have all universally felt that we got a little jipped-out, but in our conversations the story is always the same:

"Hey Dad, how come grandpa didn't speak to you in the language of his homeland?"

"He swore at me in that language and told me that was all I needed to know."

"Really Dad?."

"Listen, our parents wanted us to speak English, they wanted us to blend in, and they wanted us kids to have all the opportunities available to Americans. They wanted us to think, act and be Americans. They didn't come here to be European Americans; they came here to be Americans."

How many illegal aliens coming across the border think this way?

How many of our Blue Camp friends would call us racist for promoting this kind of thinking?

Today, we have an uncontrolled influx of illegal aliens who do not come here to embrace our historic culture but to get a "free ride." A large political constituency has hitched its success to their empowerment.

Can we possibly expect Americans dedicated to our original heritage to tolerate this onslaught; without defying the dictatorial rule that will force them to pay for entitlements this new group will be availed?

Plenty of homegrown Americans have become part of this entitlement structure and support construction of the nanny State. While American originalists (people like our grandparents) continue to pay the debt incurred in this nanny state degeneration, our new immigrants are losing the opportunities availed when freedom is available to all.

American originalists hold in contempt these developments and like their ancestors before them:

…all experience hath shewn that mankind are more disposed to suffer, while evils are sufferable than to right themselves by abolishing the forms to which they are accustomed. But when a long train of abuses and usurpations, pursuing invariably the same Object evinces a design to reduce them under absolute Despotism…

And of course that was followed with:

…it is their right, it is their duty, to throw off such Government, and to provide new Guards for their future security.

Hmmm, how much more of this do we think the American originalists might tolerate before, "abolishing the forms to which *we* are accustomed"?

While Blue Camp members are promoting the nanny State and encouraging the influx of illegal aliens, believing they will bring numbers to their cause, they are agitating *real* Americans who despise the destruction of their culture.

Today America's illegal aliens are being told to put out their hands, and if they vote for the Blue guy, the government will put money into them.

How many more hands can the United States government afford to fill?

We are already passed the tipping point yet our ship has stubbornly refused to flip.

Chalk it up to American defiance. The same defiance Americans have used to resist sufferable evils is defiance that encourages them not to abolish the *forms to which they have become accustomed*.

Americans will abolish these forms because at his core the American originalist loves freedom, he loves liberty, and he knows it is his duty to restore these rights when they have been usurped. It is his duty in serving his countrymen, and it is his duty in serving God.

I know because I am an American.

RSC Flag   by Paige

It seems if we have a new Nation, a Red State Coalition, we are going to need a new flag. In deference to our Founders, we believe only small changes to the United States Flag are necessary.

Our flag was designed by considering the primary principles of freedom, liberty and justice for all. Our only desire for secession is to restore and to protect those principles, and once again guarantee them to our people.

We propose the thirteen stripes and blue field to remain as they are. We further propose that a single white star be placed within the blue field for each State in our Coalition. Unlike our United States Flag, these stars will not be placed to take up all of the space within the blue field, but they will be equally and orderly spaced line after line leaving a line and a half empty at the bottom of the blue field.

This empty space will represent our Coalition's willingness and desire to admit any new state wishing to embrace and protect the concepts of freedom and liberty as envisioned by America's original Founders.

The Government We Deserve <small>by AHC</small>

Benjamin Franklin said, *"Those who would give up essential liberty to purchase a little temporary safety deserve neither liberty nor safety."*

It is impossible to argue that Americans enjoy unfettered liberty witnessing our government's willingness to more progressively assault our earnings and our freedoms. It is also difficult to imagine how we might gain back our liberties without deviating from our established political process.

Acknowledging the "pedestrian" American and those "dim-wits" among us not in possession of "scholarly knowledge" and the "enlightened" wisdom of those in the "educated" class; even us "knuckle-draggers" recognize obscene hypocrisy when our noses are rubbed in it.

We see that our freedom of religion, speech, and self-defense are under attack. We see our government endeavoring to limit our choices in automobiles and in food (meat is so yesterday). We see them dictate that our thermostats shouldn't be set lower than seventy-eight degrees. We see them mandate that toilet tanks only hold 1.6 gallons so we have to flush two or three times to make sure they really drain. We see most importantly, that those possessing political power desire that we do not do as we please, but as they say.

Meanwhile, our political elites fly in jumbo jets, pumping more CO_2 into the air in one trip than most of us will in a lifetime. They get "limoed" around in twelve thousand pound vehicles that get about seven miles to the gallon. They eat hundred dollar a pound steaks on *our* dime, and they keep *their* thermostats at seventy-two degrees.

They then make decisions that won't allow us to live a similar lifestyle. These monumental choices are too big for regular folk, and if left to us, the polar bears will go extinct, the third world will live in poverty (because we "steal" their energy), and California will fall into the ocean. We are smart enough to elect these leaders, but too dumb to choose our own health care.

The United States of America is exactly where it belongs; we have traded essential liberty for temporary safety and comfort. We have bought into FDR's thinking that we should be free from want and fear and we've empowered our government to limit our speech, to assault our faith, and to change our culture.

We are not the sturdy rugged individualists who built this nation; too many of us are whiners and wimps ready to let someone else take care of us.

We need to be outspoken, we need to preserve our natural rights given to us by God, not by government, and we need to be armed and prepared to protect ourselves and our countrymen from any force or from any foe.

We need to maintain the lion's share of our works for our own life improvements and for the improvements of our families. We need to forge strong alliances with like-minded Americans who believe America's law has been evaded to benefit the politically connected and the lazy. We need to be prepared to withhold our tax revenue from the Federal Government and we need to be prepared to resist military power. This can only be accomplished if many states will bind together and draw a line in the sand.

The politicians will not look kindly onto our endeavor and will attack us mercilessly, labeling us traitors and criminals, and they will use propaganda, the media, and every bit of government power they have to squash us and imprison us.

Again, Benjamin Franklin, *"We must, indeed, all hang together, or most assuredly we shall all hang separately."*

The politicians who control us only number some 500 and yet they hold under their will the future of some 300 million.

They choose to betray our culture and our inalienable rights and they aim to make simple men and women subservient to them.

If we won't fight, if we don't threaten to build a new nation in the spirit of those turbulent ancestors who dressed up like Indians and dumped tea into Boston harbor, then we deserve the government we have and we will indenture our children to the will of mortal and evil men.

Don't take our word for it:

"Freedom is never more than one generation away from extinction. We didn't pass it to our children in the bloodstream. It must be fought for, protected, and handed on for them to do the same." - Ronald Reagan

A call to action:

"It does not require a majority to prevail, but rather an irate, tireless minority keen to set brush fires in people's minds." - Sam Adams

Liberty or Tyranny   by KMP

In <u>Liberty and Tyranny</u>, Mark Levin's supreme bestseller, Levin gives the reader a terrific explanation of the statist agenda and he explains how and why statist thinking is incompatible with citizen liberties. He also explains how the United States of America has run a long way down the statist track.

Levin's little tome, diminutive in its size, is enormous in its message: if Liberty is to be preserved, it will only be through application of our Founder's principles. If these principles are not fought for and protected, then Tyranny will result.

If every single Senator, every single Representative, if all the Supreme Court, and the President himself were replaced with men and women hostile to Statist thinking, we would still be faced with dismantling an overbearing and tyrannical bureaucracy constructed of public "servants" who often maintain their positions their entire working life. These "servants" do not excel when there is liberty, their good fortune and power comes with application of the authority given to them due to their position within government. It is doubtful they will voluntarily give up their entrenched power through any legislation that could take place during one or two terms, even if we could manage to elect public officials all of like mind.

The two-state solution is in no way hostile to our Founding principles; we not only believe that this is the fastest way back to our ideals, but it is the only way.

Our Federal Government is broken, and fixing it means convincing the people who inhabit it to voluntarily give up their power and their influence. If they were people of accomplishment, honor and virtue, they might, but we know that too many of them are not. They are only in the political game to get what they can get, and the few good ones who are there for the right reasons get a bad name for their association—when you lie down with dogs, you wake up with fleas!

Do enough Americans feel enough injury to leave a union determined to subjugate the natural laws of God, to subdue the individual spirit, and to make all people subservient to the State, or are we willing to tolerate Tyranny for just a little while longer?

A united Red State Coalition movement will be a powerful rod to strike the statist down.

"When the people fear government there is Tyranny, when the government fears the people there is Liberty."   -Thomas Jefferson

Until our fear is alleviated, we shall continue to reside under Tyranny.

A New Declaration

Today, the inhabitants of America are subjugated by a Monarchial ruling class, ostensibly, of our citizens' own appointment. This body prescribes law the pedestrian among us must follow, and yet, this elitist group inoculates itself from such law, and bestows upon itself such beneficial favor, King George himself would blush with embarrassment.

How many among us would trade the tyrannical government of mother England, requesting only a few cents for each dollar we spent on tea for the arrogant monstrosity we have today which demands many of us work more than six months of each year, serving the State, before one dime shall be considered our own property?

Reviewing America's Declaration of Independence and Jefferson's list of injuries and insults suffered by our colonies at the hand of Britain to compel our separation, one leaves thinking those colonists were quite a sensitive bunch; for how would they react, faced with the insults and injuries contemporary Americans endure, under the weight of a federal government which progressively, systematically, and deliberately betrays our Constitutional freedoms and protections for its own aggrandizement?

As Jefferson did, let us list the assaults that would compel the contemporary patriot to throw off this despotic regime and reclaim again those inalienable rights guaranteed by God—among those, Life, Liberty, and the Pursuit of Happiness.

This government and its mini-Kings have destroyed State sovereignty, compelling the States to accept laws they have had no hand in making with no prescription in the Constitution for such action.

They have betrayed the very fiber of our core culture by elevating the rights and outcomes of arbitrary groups and corporations above those of individuals, creating law to favor these groups at the individual's expense.

They have assigned their law-making duties to anonymous agencies, assigning them enforcement powers, and yet these agencies are unanswerable to the electorate and immune to its wrath.

They have repeatedly and consistently been subject to little or no liability when breaking laws which would leave the average working citizen imprisoned.

They have secured for themselves lifetime pensions on the taxpayer's back for a mere two years of service.

They have secured for themselves pay increases, without taxpayer approval.

They have secured for themselves medical coverage separate from taxpayers, yet paid for by taxpayers.

They have stolen from our citizens by debasing our currency and amassing debt that is impossible to satisfy.

They have put our military personnel into harm's way and then prosecuted them for war crimes to meet political goals.

They have subverted our supreme law by bowing to international organizations.

They have encouraged our people to separate from God, to embrace fallacious philosophies obscene to the Almighty and obscene to our founding. When written, the 1st Amendment was set to protect religion from government intervention; it has been turned on its head to stop religion from influencing government, giving government a free hand in the destruction of religion.

They have demanded that secular thought be taught in our schools proclaiming it scientific, while promoting God and religion as folly.

They have undercut Constitutional protections by legislating against our right to free speech and against our right to bear arms.

They have, through judicial fiat, interpreted *public use* as equal to *political whim* and enabled government at any level to confiscate private property.

They have definitively engaged in a course to transfer power away from America's citizens to those in elected office.

They have ignored the tenth Amendment, *"The powers not delegated to the United States by the Constitution, nor prohibited by it to the States, are reserved to the States respectively, or to the people"* and seized power at every turn without consent of the states or the people.

They have endeavored to subvert the Constitution of the United States, the Constitution they took oaths to protect.

Signed—Americans of the Red State Coalition

IN CONGRESS, JULY 4, 1776
The unanimous Declaration of the thirteen united States of America

When in the Course of human events it becomes necessary for one people to dissolve the political bands which have connected them with another and to assume among the powers of the earth, the separate and equal station to which the Laws of Nature and of Nature's God entitle them, a decent respect to the opinions of mankind requires that they should declare the causes which impel them to the separation.

We hold these truths to be self-evident, that all men are created equal, that they are endowed by their Creator with certain unalienable Rights, that among these are Life, Liberty and the pursuit of Happiness. — That to secure these rights, Governments are instituted among Men, deriving their just powers from the consent of the governed, — That whenever any Form of Government becomes destructive of these ends, it is the Right of the People to alter or to abolish it, and to institute new Government, laying its foundation on such principles and organizing its powers in such form, as to them shall seem most likely to effect their Safety and Happiness. Prudence, indeed, will dictate that Governments long established should not be changed for light and transient causes; and accordingly all experience hath shewn that mankind are more disposed to suffer, while evils are sufferable than to right themselves by abolishing the forms to which they are accustomed. But when a long train of abuses and usurpations, pursuing invariably the same Object evinces a design to reduce them under absolute Despotism, it is their right, it is their duty, to throw off such Government, and to provide new

Guards for their future security. — Such has been the patient sufferance of these Colonies; and such is now the necessity which constrains them to alter their former Systems of Government. The history of the present King of Great Britain is a history of repeated injuries and usurpations, all having in direct object the establishment of an absolute Tyranny over these States. To prove this, let Facts be submitted to a candid world.

He has refused his Assent to Laws, the most wholesome and necessary for the public good.

He has forbidden his Governors to pass Laws of immediate and pressing importance, unless suspended in their operation till his Assent should be obtained; and when so suspended, he has utterly neglected to attend to them.

He has refused to pass other Laws for the accommodation of large districts of people, unless those people would relinquish the right of Representation in the Legislature, a right inestimable to them and formidable to tyrants only.

He has called together legislative bodies at places unusual, uncomfortable, and distant from the depository of their Public Records, for the sole purpose of fatiguing them into compliance with his measures.

He has dissolved Representative Houses repeatedly, for opposing with manly firmness his invasions on the rights of the people.

He has refused for a long time, after such dissolutions, to cause others to be elected, whereby the Legislative Powers, incapable of Annihilation, have returned to the People at large for their exercise; the State remaining in the mean time exposed to all the dangers of invasion from without, and convulsions within.

He has endeavoured to prevent the population of these States; for that purpose obstructing the Laws for Naturalization of Foreigners; refusing to pass others to encourage their migrations hither, and raising the conditions of new Appropriations of Lands.

He has obstructed the Administration of Justice by refusing his Assent to Laws for establishing Judiciary Powers.

He has made Judges dependent on his Will alone for the tenure of their offices, and the amount and payment of their salaries.

He has erected a multitude of New Offices, and sent hither swarms of Officers to harass our people and eat out their substance.

He has kept among us, in times of peace, Standing Armies without the Consent of our legislatures.

He has affected to render the Military independent of and superior to the Civil Power.

He has combined with others to subject us to a jurisdiction foreign to our constitution, and unacknowledged by our laws; giving his Assent to their Acts of pretended Legislation:

For quartering large bodies of armed troops among us:
For protecting them, by a mock Trial from punishment for any Murders which they should commit on the Inhabitants of these States:

For cutting off our Trade with all parts of the world:
For imposing Taxes on us without our Consent:
For depriving us in many cases, of the benefit of Trial by Jury:
For transporting us beyond Seas to be tried for pretended offences:
For abolishing the free System of English Laws in a neighbouring Province, establishing therein an Arbitrary government, and enlarging its Boundaries so as to render it at once an example and fit instrument for introducing the same absolute rule into these Colonies
For taking away our Charters, abolishing our most valuable Laws and altering fundamentally the Forms of our Governments:
For suspending our own Legislatures, and declaring themselves invested with power to legislate for us in all cases whatsoever.

He has abdicated Government here, by declaring us out of his Protection and waging War against us.

He has plundered our seas, ravaged our coasts, burnt our towns, and destroyed the lives of our people.

He is at this time transporting large Armies of foreign Mercenaries to compleat the works of death, desolation, and tyranny, already begun with circumstances of Cruelty & Perfidy scarcely paralleled in the most barbarous ages, and totally unworthy the Head of a civilized nation.

He has constrained our fellow Citizens taken Captive on the high Seas to bear Arms against their Country, to become the executioners of their friends and Brethren, or to fall themselves by their Hands.

He has excited domestic insurrections amongst us, and has endeavoured to bring on the inhabitants of our frontiers, the merciless Indian Savages whose known rule of warfare, is an undistinguished destruction of all ages, sexes and conditions.

In every stage of these Oppressions We have Petitioned for Redress in the most humble terms: Our repeated Petitions have been answered only by repeated injury. A Prince, whose character is thus marked by every act which may define a Tyrant, is unfit to be the ruler of a free people.

Nor have We been wanting in attentions to our British brethren. We have warned them from time to time of attempts by their legislature to extend an unwarrantable jurisdiction over us. We have reminded them of the circumstances of our emigration and settlement here. We have appealed to their native justice and magnanimity, and we have conjured them by the ties of our common kindred to disavow these usurpations, which would inevitably interrupt our connections and correspondence. They too have been deaf to the voice of justice and of consanguinity. We must, therefore, acquiesce in the necessity, which denounces our Separation, and hold them, as we hold the rest of mankind, Enemies in War, in Peace Friends.

We, therefore, the Representatives of the united States of America, in General Congress, Assembled, appealing to the Supreme Judge of the world for the rectitude of our intentions, do, in the Name, and by Authority of the good People of these Colonies, solemnly publish and declare, That these united Colonies are, and of Right ought to be Free and Independent States, that they are Absolved from all Allegiance to the British Crown, and that all political connection between them and the

State of Great Britain, is and ought to be totally dissolved; and that as Free and Independent States, they have full Power to levy War, conclude Peace, contract Alliances, establish Commerce, and to do all other Acts and Things which Independent States may of right do. — And for the support of this Declaration, with a firm reliance on the protection of Divine Providence, we mutually pledge to each other our Lives, our Fortunes, and our sacred Honor.

— John Hancock

New Hampshire:
Josiah Bartlett, William Whipple, Matthew Thornton

Massachusetts:
John Hancock, Samuel Adams, John Adams, Robert Treat Paine, Elbridge Gerry

Rhode Island:
Stephen Hopkins, William Ellery

Connecticut:
Roger Sherman, Samuel Huntington, William Williams, Oliver Wolcott

New York:
William Floyd, Philip Livingston, Francis Lewis, Lewis Morris

New Jersey:
Richard Stockton, John Witherspoon, Francis Hopkinson, John Hart, Abraham Clark

Pennsylvania:
Robert Morris, Benjamin Rush, Benjamin Franklin, John Morton, George Clymer, James Smith, George Taylor, James Wilson, George Ross

Delaware:
Caesar Rodney, George Read, Thomas McKean

Maryland:
Samuel Chase, William Paca, Thomas Stone, Charles Carroll of Carrollton

Virginia:
George Wythe, Richard Henry Lee, Thomas Jefferson, Benjamin Harrison, Thomas Nelson, Jr., Francis Lightfoot Lee, Carter Braxton

North Carolina:
William Hooper, Joseph Hewes, John Penn

South Carolina:
Edward Rutledge, Thomas Heyward, Jr., Thomas Lynch, Jr., Arthur Middleton

Georgia:
Button Gwinnett, Lyman Hall, George Walton

Constitution of the United States
(Unread by current politicians)

We the People of the United States, in Order to form a more perfect Union, establish Justice, insure domestic Tranquility, provide for the common defence, promote the general Welfare, and secure the Blessings of Liberty to ourselves and our Posterity, do ordain and establish this Constitution for the United States of America.

Article I
Section 1. All legislative Powers herein granted shall be vested in a Congress of the United States, which shall consist of a Senate and House of Representatives.

Section 2. The House of Representatives shall be composed of Members chosen every second Year by the People of the several States, and the Electors in each State shall have the Qualifications requisite for Electors of the most numerous Branch of the State Legislature.

No Person shall be a Representative who shall not have attained to the age of twenty five Years, and been seven Years a Citizen of the United States, and who shall not, when elected, be an Inhabitant of that State in which he shall be chosen.

Representatives and direct Taxes shall be apportioned among the several States which may be included within this Union, according to their respective Numbers, which shall be determined by adding to the whole Number of free Persons, including those bound to Service for a Term of Years, and excluding Indians not taxed, three fifths of all other Persons. The actual Enumeration shall be made within three Years after the first Meeting of the Congress of the United States, and within every subsequent Term of ten Years, in such Manner as they shall by Law direct. The Number of Representatives shall not exceed one for every thirty Thousand, but each State shall have at Least one Representative; and until such enumeration shall be made, the State of New Hampshire shall be entitled to chuse three, Massachusetts eight, Rhode-Island and Providence Plantations one, Connecticut five, New-York six, New Jersey four, Pennsylvania eight, Delaware one, Maryland six, Virginia ten, North Carolina five, South Carolina five, and Georgia three.

When vacancies happen in the Representation from any State, the Executive Authority thereof shall issue Writs of Election to fill such Vacancies.

The House of Representatives shall chuse their Speaker and other Officers; and shall have the sole Power of Impeachment.

Section 3. The Senate of the United States shall be composed of two Senators from each State, chosen by the Legislature thereof, for six Years; and each Senator shall have one Vote.

Immediately after they shall be assembled in Consequence of the first Election, they shall be divided as equally as may be into three Classes. The Seats of the Senators of the first Class shall be vacated at the Expiration of the second Year, of the second Class at the Expiration of the fourth Year, and the third Class at the Expiration of the sixth Year, so that one third may be chosen every second Year; and if Vacancies happen by Resignation, or otherwise, during the Recess of the Legislature of any State, the Executive thereof may make temporary Appointments until the next Meeting of the Legislature, which shall then fill such Vacancies.

No Person shall be a Senator who shall not have attained to the Age of thirty Years, and been nine Years a Citizen of the United States and who shall not, when elected, be an Inhabitant of that State for which he shall be chosen.

The Vice President of the United States shall be President of the Senate, but shall have no Vote, unless they be equally divided.

The Senate shall chuse their other Officers, and also a President pro tempore, in the Absence of the Vice President, or when he shall exercise the Office of President of the United States.

The Senate shall have the sole Power to try all Impeachments. When sitting for that Purpose, they shall be on Oath or Affirmation. When the President of the United States is tried, the Chief Justice shall preside: And no Person shall be convicted without the Concurrence of two thirds of the Members present.

Judgment in Cases of Impeachment shall not extend further than to removal from Office, and disqualification to hold and enjoy any Office of Honor, Trust or Profit under the United States: but the Party convicted shall nevertheless be liable and subject to Indictment, Trial, Judgment and Punishment, according to Law.

Section 4. The Times, Places and Manner of holding Elections for Senators and Representatives, shall be prescribed in each State by the Legislature thereof; but the Congress may at any time by Law make or alter such Regulations, except as to the Places of chusing Senators.

The Congress shall assemble at least once in every Year, and such Meeting shall be on the first Monday in December, unless they shall by Law appoint a different Day.

Section 5. Each House shall be the Judge of the Elections, Returns and Qualifications of its own Members, and a Majority of each shall constitute a Quorum to do Business; but a smaller Number may adjourn from day to day, and may be authorized to compel the Attendance of absent Members, in such Manner, and under such Penalties as each House may provide.

Each House may determine the Rules of its Proceedings, punish its Members for disorderly Behaviour, and, with the Concurrence of two thirds, expel a Member.

Each House shall keep a Journal of its Proceedings, and from time to time publish the same, excepting such Parts as may in their Judgment require Secrecy; and the Yeas and Nays of the Members of either House on any question shall, at the Desire of one fifth of those Present, be entered on the Journal.

Neither House, during the Session of Congress, shall, without the Consent of the other, adjourn for more than three days, nor to any other Place than that in which the two Houses shall be sitting.

Section 6. The Senators and Representatives shall receive a Compensation for their Services, to be ascertained by Law, and paid out of the Treasury of the United States. They shall in all Cases, except Treason, Felony and Breach of the Peace, be privileged from Arrest during their Attendance at the Session of their respective Houses, and in going to and returning from the same; and for any Speech or Debate in either House, they shall not be questioned in any other Place.

No Senator or Representative shall, during the Time for which he was elected, be appointed to any civil Office under the Authority of the United States, which shall have been created, or the Emoluments whereof shall have been encreased during such time: and no Person holding any Office under the United States, shall be a Member of either House during his Continuance in Office.

Section 7. All Bills for raising Revenue shall originate in the House of Representatives; but the Senate may propose or concur with Amendments as on other Bills.

Every Bill which shall have passed the House of Representatives and the Senate, shall, before it become a Law, be presented to the President of the United States; if he approve he shall sign it, but if not he shall return it, with his Objections to that House in which it shall have originated, who shall enter the Objections at large on their Journal, and proceed to reconsider it. If after such Reconsideration two thirds of that House shall agree to pass the Bill, it shall be sent, together with the Objections, to the other House, by which it shall likewise be reconsidered, and if approved by two thirds of that House, it shall become a Law. But in all such Cases the Votes of both Houses shall be determined by Yeas and Nays, and the Names of the Persons voting for and against the Bill shall be entered on the Journal of each House respectively. If any Bill shall not be returned by the President within ten Days (Sundays excepted) after it shall have been presented to him, the Same shall be a Law, in like Manner as if he had signed it, unless the Congress by their Adjournment prevent its Return, in which Case it shall not be a Law.

Every Order, Resolution, or Vote to which the Concurrence of the Senate and House of Representatives may be necessary (except on a question of Adjournment) shall be presented to the President of the United States; and before the Same shall take Effect, shall be approved by him, or being disapproved by him, shall be repassed by two thirds of the Senate and House of Representatives, according to the Rules and Limitations prescribed in the Case of a Bill.

Section 8. The Congress shall have Power To lay and collect Taxes, Duties, Imposts and Excises, to pay the Debts and provide for the common Defence and general Welfare of the United States; but all Duties, Imposts and Excises shall be uniform throughout the United States;

To borrow Money on the credit of the United States;

To regulate Commerce with foreign Nations, and among the several States, and with the Indian Tribes;

To establish an uniform Rule of Naturalization, and uniform Laws on the subject of Bankruptcies throughout the United States;

To coin Money, regulate the Value thereof, and of foreign Coin, and fix the Standard of Weights and Measures;

To provide for the Punishment of counterfeiting the Securities and current Coin of the United States;

To establish Post Offices and post Roads;

To promote the Progress of Science and useful Arts, by securing for limited Times to Authors and Inventors the exclusive Right to their respective Writings and Discoveries;

To constitute Tribunals inferior to the supreme Court;

To define and punish Piracies and Felonies committed on the high Seas, and Offences against the Law of Nations;

To declare War, grant Letters of Marque and Reprisal, and make Rules concerning Captures on Land and Water;

To raise and support Armies, but no Appropriation of Money to that Use shall be for a longer Term than two Years;

To provide and maintain a Navy;

To make Rules for the Government and Regulation of the land and naval Forces;

To provide for calling forth the Militia to execute the Laws of the Union, suppress Insurrections and repel Invasions;

To provide for organizing, arming, and disciplining, the Militia, and for governing such Part of them as may be employed in the

Service of the United States, reserving to the States respectively, the Appointment of the Officers, and the Authority of training the Militia according to the discipline prescribed by Congress;

To exercise exclusive Legislation in all Cases whatsoever, over such District (not exceeding ten Miles square) as may, by Cession of particular States, and the Acceptance of Congress, become the Seat of the Government of the United States, and to exercise like Authority over all Places purchased by the Consent of the Legislature of the State in which the Same shall be, for the Erection of Forts, Magazines, Arsenals, dock-Yards, and other needful Buildings;--And

To make all Laws which shall be necessary and proper for carrying into Execution the foregoing Powers, and all other Powers vested by this Constitution in the Government of the United States, or in any Department or Officer thereof.

Section 9. The Migration or Importation of such Persons as any of the States now existing shall think proper to admit, shall not be prohibited by the Congress prior to the Year one thousand eight hundred and eight, but a Tax or duty may be imposed on such Importation, not exceeding ten dollars for each Person.

The Privilege of the Writ of Habeas Corpus shall not be suspended, unless when in Cases of Rebellion or Invasion the public Safety may require it.

No Bill of Attainder or ex post facto Law shall be passed.

No Capitation, or other direct, Tax shall be laid, unless in Proportion to the Census or Enumeration herein before directed to be taken.

No Tax or Duty shall be laid on Articles exported from any State.

No Preference shall be given by any Regulation of Commerce or Revenue to the Ports of one State over those of another: nor shall Vessels bound to, or from, one State, be obliged to enter, clear or pay Duties in another.

No Money shall be drawn from the Treasury, but in Consequence of Appropriations made by Law; and a regular Statement and Account of Receipts and Expenditures of all public Money shall be published from time to time.

No Title of Nobility shall be granted by the United States: And no Person holding any Office of Profit or Trust under them, shall, without the Consent of the Congress, accept of any present, Emolument, Office, or Title, of any kind whatever, from any King, Prince, or foreign State.

Section 10. No State shall enter into any Treaty, Alliance, or Confederation; grant Letters of Marque and Reprisal; coin Money; emit Bills of Credit; make any Thing but gold and silver Coin a Tender in Payment of Debts; pass any Bill of Attainder, ex post facto Law, or Law impairing the Obligation of Contracts, or grant any Title of Nobility.

No State shall, without the Consent of the Congress, lay any Imposts or Duties on Imports or Exports, except what may be absolutely necessary for executing it's inspection Laws: and the net Produce of all Duties and Imposts, laid by any State on Imports or Exports, shall be for the Use of the Treasury of the United States; and all such Laws shall be subject to the Revision and Controul of the Congress.

No State shall, without the Consent of Congress, lay any Duty of Tonnage, keep Troops, or Ships of War in time of Peace, enter into any Agreement or Compact with another State, or with a foreign Power, or engage in War, unless actually invaded, or in such imminent Danger as will not admit of delay.

Article II
Section 1. The executive Power shall be vested in a President of the United States of America. He shall hold his Office during the Term of four Years, and, together with the Vice President, chosen for the same Term, be elected, as follows:

Each State shall appoint, in such Manner as the Legislature thereof may direct, a Number of Electors, equal to the whole Number of Senators and Representatives to which the State may be entitled in the Congress: but no Senator or Representative, or Person holding an Office of Trust or Profit under the United States, shall be appointed an Elector.

The Electors shall meet in their respective States, and vote by Ballot for two Persons, of whom one at least shall not be an Inhabitant of the same State with themselves. And they shall make a List of all the Persons voted for, and of the Number of Votes for each; which List they shall sign and certify, and transmit sealed to the Seat of the Government of the United States, directed to the President of the Senate. The President of the Senate shall, in the Presence of the Senate and House of Representatives, open all the Certificates, and the Votes shall then be counted. The Person having the greatest Number of Votes shall be the President, if such Number be a Majority of the whole Number of Electors appointed; and if there be more than one who have such Majority, and have an equal Number of Votes, then the House of Representatives shall immediately chuse by Ballot one of them for President; and if no Person have a Majority, then from the five highest on the List the said House shall in like Manner chuse the President. But in chusing the President, the Votes shall be taken by States, the Representation from each State having one Vote; A quorum for this Purpose shall consist of a Member or Members from two thirds of the States, and a Majority of all the States shall be necessary to a Choice. In every Case, after the Choice of the President, the Person having the greatest Number of Votes of the Electors shall be the Vice President. But if there should remain two or more who have equal Votes, the Senate shall chuse from them by Ballot the Vice President.

The Congress may determine the Time of chusing the Electors, and the Day on which they shall give their Votes; which Day shall be the same throughout the United States.

No Person except a natural born Citizen, or a Citizen of the United States, at the time of the Adoption of this Constitution, shall be eligible to the Office of President; neither shall any Person be eligible to that Office who shall not have attained to the Age of thirty five Years, and been fourteen Years a Resident within the United States.

In Case of the Removal of the President from Office, or of his Death, Resignation, or Inability to discharge the Powers and Duties of the said Office, the Same shall devolve on the Vice President, and the Congress may by Law provide for the Case of Removal, Death, Resignation or Inability, both of the President and Vice President, declaring what Officer shall then act as President, and such Officer shall act accordingly, until the Disability be removed, or a President shall be elected.

The President shall, at stated Times, receive for his Services, a Compensation, which shall neither be encreased nor diminished during the Period for which he shall have been elected, and he shall not receive within that Period any other Emolument from the United States, or any of them.

Before he enter on the Execution of his Office, he shall take the following Oath or Affirmation:--"I do solemnly swear (or affirm) that I will faithfully execute the Office of President of the United States, and will to the best of my Ability, preserve, protect and defend the Constitution of the United States."

Section 2. The President shall be Commander in Chief of the Army and Navy of the United States, and of the Militia of the several States, when called into the actual Service of the United States; he may require the Opinion, in writing, of the principal Officer in each of the executive Departments, upon any Subject relating to the Duties of their respective Offices, and he shall have Power to grant Reprieves and Pardons for Offences against the United States, except in Cases of Impeachment.

He shall have Power, by and with the Advice and Consent of the Senate, to make Treaties, provided two thirds of the Senators present concur; and he shall nominate, and by and with the Advice and Consent of the Senate, shall appoint Ambassadors, other public Ministers and Consuls, Judges of the supreme Court, and all other Officers of the United States, whose Appointments are not herein otherwise provided for, and which shall be established by Law: but the Congress may by Law vest the Appointment of such inferior Officers, as they think proper, in the President alone, in the Courts of Law, or in the Heads of Departments.

The President shall have Power to fill up all Vacancies that may happen during the Recess of the Senate, by granting Commissions which shall expire at the End of their next Session.

Section 3. He shall from time to time give to the Congress Information of the State of the Union, and recommend to their Consideration such Measures as he shall judge necessary and expedient; he may, on extraordinary Occasions, convene both Houses, or either of them, and in Case of Disagreement between them, with Respect to the Time of Adjournment, he may adjourn them to such Time as he shall think proper; he shall receive Ambassadors and other public Ministers; he shall take Care that the Laws be faithfully executed, and shall Commission all the Officers of the United States.

Section 4. The President, Vice President and all civil Officers of the United States, shall be removed from Office on Impeachment for, and Conviction of, Treason, Bribery, or other high Crimes and Misdemeanors.

Article III
Section 1. The judicial Power of the United States, shall be vested in one supreme Court, and in such inferior Courts as the Congress may from time to time ordain and establish. The Judges, both of the supreme and inferior Courts, shall hold their Offices during good Behaviour, and shall, at stated Times, receive for their Services, a Compensation, which shall not be diminished during their Continuance in Office.

Section 2. The judicial Power shall extend to all Cases, in Law and Equity, arising under this Constitution, the Laws of the United States, and Treaties made, or which shall be made, under their Authority;--to all Cases affecting Ambassadors, other public Ministers and Consuls;--to all Cases of admiralty and maritime Jurisdiction;--to Controversies to which the United States shall be a Party;--to Controversies between two or more States;--between a State and Citizens of another State;--between Citizens of different States;--between Citizens of the same State claiming Lands under Grants of different States, and between a State, or the Citizens thereof, and foreign States, Citizens or Subjects.

In all Cases affecting Ambassadors, other public Ministers and Consuls, and those in which a State shall be Party, the supreme Court shall have original Jurisdiction. In all the other Cases before mentioned, the supreme Court shall have appellate Jurisdiction, both as to Law and Fact, with such Exceptions, and under such Regulations as the Congress shall make.

The Trial of all Crimes, except in Cases of Impeachment, shall be by Jury; and such Trial shall be held in the State where the said Crimes shall have been committed; but when not committed within any State, the Trial shall be at such Place or Places as the Congress may by Law have directed.

Section 3. Treason against the United States, shall consist only in levying War against them, or in adhering to their Enemies, giving them Aid and Comfort. No Person shall be convicted of Treason unless on the Testimony of two Witnesses to the same overt Act, or on Confession in open Court.

The Congress shall have Power to declare the Punishment of Treason, but no Attainder of Treason shall work Corruption of Blood, or Forfeiture except during the Life of the Person attainted.

Article IV
Section 1. Full Faith and Credit shall be given in each State to the public Acts, Records, and judicial Proceedings of every other State. And the Congress may by general Laws prescribe the Manner in which such Acts, Records, and Proceedings shall be proved, and the Effect thereof.

Section 2. The Citizens of each State shall be entitled to all Privileges and Immunities of Citizens in the several States.

A Person charged in any State with Treason, Felony, or other Crime, who shall flee from Justice, and be found in another State, shall on Demand of the executive Authority of the State from which he fled, be delivered up, to be removed to the State having Jurisdiction of the Crime.

No Person held to Service or Labour in one State, under the Laws thereof, escaping into another, shall, in Consequence of any Law or Regulation therein, be discharged from such Service or Labour, but shall be delivered up on Claim of the Party to whom such Service or Labour may be due.

Section 3. New States may be admitted by the Congress into this Union; but no new States shall be formed or erected within the Jurisdiction of any other State; nor any State be formed by the Junction of two or more States, or Parts of States, without the

Consent of the Legislatures of the States concerned as well as of the Congress.

The Congress shall have Power to dispose of and make all needful Rules and Regulations respecting the Territory or other Property belonging to the United States; and nothing in this Constitution shall be so construed as to Prejudice any Claims of the United States, or of any particular State.

Section 4. The United States shall guarantee to every State in this Union a Republican Form of Government, and shall protect each of them against Invasion; and on Application of the Legislature, or of the Executive (when the Legislature cannot be convened) against domestic Violence.

Article V
The Congress, whenever two thirds of both Houses shall deem it necessary, shall propose Amendments to this Constitution, or, on the Application of the Legislatures of two thirds of the several States, shall call a Convention for proposing Amendments, which, in either Case, shall be valid to all Intents and Purposes, as Part of this Constitution, when ratified by the Legislatures of three fourths of the several States, or by Conventions in three fourths thereof, as the one or the other Mode of Ratification may be proposed by the Congress; Provided that no Amendment which may be made prior to the Year One thousand eight hundred and eight shall in any Manner affect the first and fourth Clauses in the Ninth Section of the first Article; and that no State, without its Consent, shall be deprived of its equal Suffrage in the Senate.

Article VI
All Debts contracted and Engagements entered into, before the Adoption of this Constitution, shall be as valid against the United States under this Constitution, as under the Confederation.

This Constitution, and the Laws of the United States which shall be made in Pursuance thereof; and all Treaties made, or which shall be made, under the Authority of the United States, shall be the supreme Law of the Land; and the Judges in every State shall be bound thereby, any Thing in the Constitution or Laws of any State to the Contrary notwith-standing.

The Senators and Representatives before mentioned, and the Members of the several State Legislatures, and all executive and judicial Officers, both of the United States and of the several States, shall be bound by Oath or Affirmation, to support this Constitution; but no religious Test shall ever be required as a Qualification to any Office or public Trust under the United States.

Article VII
The Ratification of the Conventions of nine States, shall be sufficient for the Establishment of this Constitution between the States so ratifying the Same.

Done in Convention by the Unanimous Consent of the States present the Seventeenth Day of September in the Year of our Lord one thousand seven hundred and Eighty seven and of the Independence of the United States of America the Twelfth

In witness whereof We have hereunto subscribed our Names,

George Washington--President and deputy from Virginia

New Hampshire: John Langdon, Nicholas Gilman

Massachusetts: Nathaniel Gorham, Rufus King

Connecticut: William Samuel Johnson, Roger Sherman

New York: Alexander Hamilton

New Jersey: William Livingston, David Brearly, William Paterson, Jonathan Dayton

Pennsylvania: Benjamin Franklin, Thomas Mifflin, Robert Morris, George Clymer, Thomas FitzSimons, Jared Ingersoll, James Wilson, Gouverneur Morris

Delaware: George Read, Gunning Bedford, Jr., John Dickinson, Richard Bassett, Jacob Broom

Maryland: James McHenry, Daniel of Saint Thomas Jenifer, Daniel Carroll

Virginia: John Blair, James Madison, Jr.

North Carolina: William Blount, Richard Dobbs Spaight, Hugh Williamson

South Carolina: John Rutledge, Charles Cotesworth Pinckney, Charles Pinckney, Pierce Butler

Georgia: William Few, Abraham Baldwin

Amendment 1

Congress shall make no law respecting an establishment of religion, or prohibiting the free exercise thereof; or abridging the freedom of speech, or of the press; or the right of the people peaceably to assemble, and to petition the government for a redress of grievances.

Amendment 2

A well regulated militia, being necessary to the security of a free state, the right of the people to keep and bear arms, shall not be infringed.

Amendment 3

No soldier shall, in time of peace be quartered in any house, without the consent of the owner, nor in time of war, but in a manner to be prescribed by law.

Amendment 4

The right of the people to be secure in their persons, houses, papers, and effects, against unreasonable searches and seizures, shall not be violated, and no warrants shall issue, but upon probable cause, supported by oath or affirmation, and particularly describing the place to be searched, and the persons or things to be seized.

Amendment 5

No person shall be held to answer for a capital, or otherwise infamous crime, unless on a presentment or indictment of a grand jury, except in cases arising in the land or naval forces, or in the militia, when in actual service in time of war or public danger; nor shall any person be subject for the same offense to be twice put in jeopardy of life or limb; nor shall be compelled in any criminal case to be a witness against himself, nor be deprived of life, liberty, or property, without due process of law; nor shall private property be taken for public use, without just compensation.

Amendment 6

In all criminal prosecutions, the accused shall enjoy the right to a speedy and public trial, by an impartial jury of the state and district wherein the crime shall have been committed, which district shall have been previously ascertained by law, and to be informed of the nature and cause of the accusation; to be confronted with the witnesses against him; to have compulsory process for obtaining witnesses in his favor, and to have the assistance of counsel for his defense.

Amendment 7

In suits at common law, where the value in controversy shall exceed twenty dollars, the right of trial by jury shall be preserved, and no fact tried by a jury, shall be otherwise reexamined in any court of the United States, than according to the rules of the common law.

Amendment 8

Excessive bail shall not be required, nor excessive fines imposed, nor cruel and unusual punishments inflicted.

Amendment 9

The enumeration in the Constitution, of certain rights, shall not be construed to deny or disparage others retained by the people.

Amendment 10

The powers not delegated to the United States by the Constitution, nor prohibited by it to the states, are reserved to the states respectively, or to the people.

Amendment 11 (1798)

The judicial power of the United States shall not be construed to extend to any suit in law or equity, commenced or prosecuted against one of the United States by citizens of another state, or by citizens or subjects of any foreign state.

Amendment 12 (1804)

The electors shall meet in their respective states and vote by ballot for President and Vice-President, one of whom, at least, shall not be an inhabitant of the same state with themselves; they shall name in their ballots the person voted for as President, and in distinct ballots the person voted for as Vice-President, and they shall make distinct lists of all persons voted for as President, and of all persons voted for as Vice-President, and of the number of votes for each, which lists they shall sign and certify, and transmit sealed to the seat of the government of the United States, directed to the President of the Senate;--The President of the Senate shall, in the presence of the Senate and House of Representatives, open all the certificates and the votes shall then be counted;--the person having the greatest number of votes for President, shall be the President, if such number be a majority of the whole number of electors appointed; and if no person have such majority, then from the persons having the highest numbers not exceeding three on the list of those voted for as President, the House of Representatives shall choose immediately, by ballot, the President. But in choosing the President, the votes shall be taken by states, the representation from each state having one vote; a quorum for this purpose shall consist of a member or members from two-thirds of the states, and a majority of all the states shall be necessary to a choice. And if the House of Representatives shall not choose a President whenever the right of choice shall devolve upon them, before the fourth day of March next following, then the Vice-President shall act as President, as in the case of the death or other constitutional disability of the President. The person having the greatest number of votes as Vice-President, shall be the Vice-President, if such number be a majority of the whole number of electors appointed, and if no person have a majority, then from the two highest numbers on the list, the Senate shall choose the Vice-President; a quorum for the purpose shall consist of two-thirds of the whole number of Senators, and a majority of the whole number shall be necessary to a choice. But no person constitutionally ineligible to the office of President shall be eligible to that of Vice-President of the United States.

Amendment 13 (1865)

Section 1. Neither slavery nor involuntary servitude, except as a punishment for crime whereof the party shall have been duly convicted, shall exist within the United States, or any place subject to their jurisdiction.

Section 2. Congress shall have power to enforce this article by appropriate legislation.

Amendment 14 (1868)

Section 1. All persons born or naturalized in the United States, and subject to the jurisdiction thereof, are citizens of the United States and of the state wherein they reside. No state shall make or enforce any law which shall abridge the privileges or immunities of citizens of the United States; nor shall any state deprive any person of life, liberty, or property, without due process of law; nor deny to any person within its jurisdiction the equal protection of the laws.

Section 2. Representatives shall be apportioned among the several states according to their respective numbers, counting the whole number of persons in each state, excluding Indians not taxed. But when the right to vote at any election for the choice of electors for President and Vice President of the United States, Representatives in Congress, the executive and judicial officers of a state, or the members of the legislature thereof, is denied to any of the male inhabitants of such state, being twenty-one years of age, and citizens of the United States, or in any way abridged, except for participation in rebellion, or other crime, the basis of representation therein shall be reduced in the proportion which the number of such male citizens shall bear to the whole number of male citizens twenty-one years of age in such state.

Section 3. No person shall be a Senator or Representative in Congress, or elector of President and Vice President, or hold any office, civil or military, under the United States, or under any state, who, having previously taken an oath, as a member of Congress, or as an officer of the United States, or as a member of any state legislature, or as an executive or judicial officer of any state, to support the Constitution of the United States, shall have engaged in insurrection or rebellion against the same, or given aid or comfort to the enemies thereof. But Congress may by a vote of two-thirds of each house, remove such disability.

Section 4. The validity of the public debt of the United States, authorized by law, including debts incurred for payment of pensions and bounties for services in suppressing insurrection or rebellion, shall not be questioned. But neither the United States nor any state shall assume or pay any debt or obligation incurred in aid of insurrection or rebellion against the United States, or any claim for the loss or emancipation of any slave; but all such debts, obligations and claims shall be held illegal and void.

Section 5. The Congress shall have power to enforce, by appropriate legislation, the provisions of this article.
Amendment 15 (1870)

Section 1. The right of citizens of the United States to vote shall not be denied or abridged by the United States or by any state on account of race, color, or previous condition of servitude.

Section 2. The Congress shall have power to enforce this article by appropriate legislation.

Amendment 16 (1913)

The Congress shall have power to lay and collect taxes on incomes, from whatever source derived, without apportionment among the several states, and without regard to any census of enumeration.

Amendment 17 (1913)

The Senate of the United States shall be composed of two Senators from each state, elected by the people thereof, for six years; and each Senator shall have one vote. The electors in each state shall have the qualifications requisite for electors of the most numerous branch of the state legislatures.

When vacancies happen in the representation of any state in the Senate, the executive authority of such state shall issue writs of election to fill such vacancies: Provided, that the legislature of any state may empower the executive thereof to make temporary appointments until the people fill the vacancies by election as the legislature may direct.

This amendment shall not be so construed as to affect the election or term of any Senator chosen before it becomes valid as part of the Constitution.

Amendment 18 (1919)

Section 1. After one year from the ratification of this article the manufacture, sale, or transportation of intoxicating liquors within, the importation thereof into, or the exportation thereof from the United States and all territory subject to the jurisdiction thereof for beverage purposes is hereby prohibited.

Section 2. The Congress and the several states shall have concurrent power to enforce this article by appropriate legislation.

Section 3. This article shall be inoperative unless it shall have been ratified as an amendment to the Constitution by the legislatures of the several states, as provided in the Constitution, within seven years from the date of the submission hereof to the states by the Congress.

Amendment 19 (1920)

The right of citizens of the United States to vote shall not be denied or abridged by the United States or by any state on account of sex.

Congress shall have power to enforce this article by appropriate legislation.

Amendment 20 (1933)

Section 1. The terms of the President and Vice President shall end at noon on the 20th day of January, and the terms of Senators and Representatives at noon on the 3d day of January, of the years in which such terms would have ended if this article had not been ratified; and the terms of their successors shall then begin.

Section 2. The Congress shall assemble at least once in every year, and such meeting shall begin at noon on the 3d day of January, unless they shall by law appoint a different day.

Section 3. If, at the time fixed for the beginning of the term of the President, the President elect shall have died, the Vice President elect shall become President. If a President shall not have been chosen before the time fixed for the beginning of his term, or if the President elect shall have failed to qualify, then the Vice President elect shall act as President until a President shall have qualified; and the Congress may by law provide for the case wherein neither a President elect nor a Vice President elect shall have qualified, declaring who shall then act as President, or the manner in which one who is to act shall be selected, and such person shall act accordingly until a President or Vice President shall have qualified.

Section 4. The Congress may by law provide for the case of the death of any of the persons from whom the House of Representatives may choose a President whenever the right of choice shall have devolved upon them, and for the case of the death of any of the persons from whom the Senate may choose a Vice President whenever the right of choice shall have devolved upon them.

Section 5. Sections 1 and 2 shall take effect on the 15th day of October following the ratification of this article.

Section 6. This article shall be inoperative unless it shall have been ratified as an amendment to the Constitution by the legislatures of three-fourths of the several states within seven years from the date of its submission.

Amendment 21 (1933)

Section 1. The eighteenth article of amendment to the Constitution of the United States is hereby repealed.

Section 2. The transportation or importation into any state, territory, or possession of the United States for delivery or use therein of intoxicating liquors, in violation of the laws thereof, is hereby prohibited.

Section 3. This article shall be inoperative unless it shall have been ratified as an amendment to the Constitution by conventions in the several states, as provided in the Constitution, within seven years from the date of the submission hereof to the states by the Congress.

Amendment 22 (1951)

Section 1. No person shall be elected to the office of the President more than twice, and no person who has held the office of President, or acted as President, for more than two years of a term to which some other person was elected President shall be elected to the office of the President more than once. But this article shall not apply to any person holding the office of President when this article was proposed by the Congress, and shall not prevent any person who may be holding the office of President, or acting as President, during the term within which this article becomes operative from holding the office of President or acting as President during the remainder of such term.

Section 2. This article shall be inoperative unless it shall have been ratified as an amendment to the Constitution by the legislatures of three-fourths of the several states within seven years from the date of its submission to the states by the Congress.

Amendment 23 (1961)

Section 1. The District constituting the seat of government of the United States shall appoint in such manner as the Congress may direct:

A number of electors of President and Vice President equal to the whole number of Senators and Representatives in Congress to which the District would be entitled if it were a state, but in no event more than the least populous state; they shall be in addition to those appointed by the states, but they shall be considered, for the purposes of the election of President and Vice President, to be electors appointed by a state; and they shall meet in the District and perform such duties as provided by the twelfth article of amendment.

Section 2. The Congress shall have power to enforce this article by appropriate legislation.

Amendment 24 (1964)

Section 1. The right of citizens of the United States to vote in any primary or other election for President or Vice President, for electors for President or Vice President, or for Senator or Representative in Congress, shall not be denied or abridged by the United States or any state by reason of failure to pay any poll tax or other tax.

Section 2. The Congress shall have power to enforce this article by appropriate legislation.

Amendment 25 (1967)

Section 1. In case of the removal of the President from office or of his death or resignation, the Vice President shall become President.

Section 2. Whenever there is a vacancy in the office of the Vice President, the President shall nominate a Vice President who shall take office upon confirmation by a majority vote of both Houses of Congress.

Section 3. Whenever the President transmits to the President pro tempore of the Senate and the Speaker of the House of Representatives his written declaration that he is unable to discharge the powers and duties of his office, and until he transmits to them a written declaration to the contrary, such powers and duties shall be discharged by the Vice President as Acting President.

Section 4. Whenever the Vice President and a majority of either the principal officers of the executive departments or of such other body as Congress may by law provide, transmit to the President pro tempore of the Senate and the Speaker of the House of Representatives their written declaration that the President is unable to discharge the powers and duties of his office, the Vice President shall immediately assume the powers and duties of the office as Acting President.

Thereafter, when the President transmits to the President pro tempore of the Senate and the Speaker of the House of Representatives his written declaration that no inability exists, he shall resume the powers and duties of his office unless the Vice President and a majority of either the principal officers of the executive department or of such other body as Congress may by law provide, transmit within four days to the President pro tempore of the Senate and the Speaker of the House of Representatives their written declaration that the President is unable to discharge the powers and duties of his office. Thereupon Congress shall decide the issue, assembling within forty-eight hours for that purpose if not in session. If the Congress, within twenty-one days after receipt of the latter written declaration, or, if Congress is not in session, within twenty-one days after Congress is required to assemble, determines by two-thirds vote of both Houses that the President is unable to discharge the powers and duties of his office, the Vice President shall continue to discharge the same as Acting President; otherwise, the President shall resume the powers and duties of his office.

Amendment 26 (1971)

Section 1. The right of citizens of the United States, who are 18 years of age or older, to vote, shall not be denied or abridged by the United States or any state on account of age.

Section 2. The Congress shall have the power to enforce this article by appropriate legislation.

Amendment 27 (1992)

No law varying the compensation for the services of the Senators and Representatives shall take effect until an election of Representatives shall have intervened.

Notes

Generally, this portion of a manuscript is dedicated to stave off partisan assaults by an author's detractors by collating and listing the references which support his opinions and claims. A kind of preemptive defense against those poised to attack, and who would attempt to distort the veracity within a work. The exercise is designed to protect an author's credibility.

Our little group isn't too worried about its credibility and fully expects that the "educated" class will affix the labels "uneducated, dumb, and Neanderthal" to our work. We will wear these criticisms with pride.

We claim to be nothing but blue collar guys working hard to take care of our families and unhappy that our government takes so much from us making our task that much harder.

None of us felt equipped to studiously and accurately list our particular references anyway, so we decided only to list some of the books that we have read and have used in the conversations and arguments amongst ourselves.

Basic Economics	-Thomas Sowell
Applied Economics	-Thomas Sowell
Freakonomics	-Levitt and Dubner
Meltdown	-Thomas E. Woods Jr.
New Deal or Raw Deal	-Burton Folsom, Jr.
First Among Equals	-Kenneth W. Starr
Men in Black	-Mark R. Levin
Liberty and Tyranny	-Mark R. Levin
High Crimes and Misdemeanors	-Ann Coulter
Treason	-Ann Coulter
Guilty	-Ann Coulter
Bias	-Bernard Goldberg
Arrogance	-Bernard Goldberg

100 People Screwing Up America	-Bernard Goldberg
Hollywood Interrupted	-Breitbart & Ebner
Betrayal	-Linda Chavez
Fleeced	-Morris & McGann
A Bold Fresh Piece of Humanity	-Bill O'Reilly
Who's Looking out for You	-Bill O'Reilly
Culture Warrior	-Bill O'Reilly
The Way Things Ought to Be	-Rush Limbaugh
Get Off My Honor	-Hans Zeiger
Give Me a Break	-John Stossel
Real Federalism	-Michael S. Greve
Common Sense	-Paine and Beck
Commies	-Ronald Radosh
The American Ideal of 1776	-Hamilton Abert Long
The 5000 Year Leap	-W. Cleon Skousen
The Constitution	-Heritage Foundation
The Federalist Papers	-Hamilton, Madison, Jay
Alexander Hamilton, American	-Richard Brookhiser
The Real Jimmy Carter	-Steven F. Hayward
Pimps, Whores and Welfare Brats	-Starr Parker
Do as I say, Not as I do	-Peter Schweizer
Hegemony or Survival	-Noam Chomsky
P.I.G. to the South	-Clint Johnson
P.I.G. to Islam	-Robert Spencer
P.I.G. to American History	-Thomas Woods
The Entrepreneur's Manual	-Richard M. White
The Warren Buffet Way	-Robert G. Hagstrom
The Art of the Deal	-Donald Trump
The Flat Tax Revolution	-Steve Forbes
Mao	-Chang and Halliday
John Adams	-David McCullough
Truman	-David McCullough
1776	-David McCullough
Operating Manual for Spaceship Earth	-R. Buckminster Fuller
The Holy Bible	-God

"The King's cheese is half wasted in parings; but no matter, 'tis made of the peoples milk."

Benjamin Franklin